D1077859

WITHDRAWN

19/4/23

Training Needs Analysis in the Workplace

The Kogan Page Practical Trainer Series

Series Editor: Roger Buckley

PRACTICAL TRAINER SERIES

KOGAN
PAGE

Training Needs Analysis in the Workplace

ROBYN PETERSON

KOGAN PAGE
Published in association with the
Institute of Training and Development

For Bill

First published in1992

Kogan Page Limited
120 Pentonville Road
London N1 9JN

© Robyn Jayne Peterson, 1992

British Library Cataloguing in Publication Data

A CIP record of this book is available from the British Library.

ISBN 0 7494 0546 5

Typeset by Koinonia Ltd, Bury
Printed and bound in Great Britain by Biddles Ltd, Guildford and King's Lynn

Contents

Series Editor's Foreword

Organizations get things done when people do their jobs effectively. To make this happen they need to be well trained. A number of people are likely to be involved in this training: identifying the needs of the organization and of the individual, selecting or designing appropriate training to meet those needs, delivering it and assessing how effective it was. It is not only 'professional' or full-time trainers who are involved in this process; personnel managers, line managers, supervisors and job holders are all likely to have a part to play.

This series has been written for all those who get involved with training in some way or another, whether they are senior personnel managers trying to link the goals of the organization with training needs or job holders who have been given responsibility for training newcomers. Therefore, the series is essentially a practical one which focuses on specific aspects of the training function. This book is the eleventh to be published in the series, which has become so popular that it is intended to include additional volumes whenever a need is found for practical guidelines in some area of training. This is not to say that the theoretical underpinnings of the practical aspects of training are unimportant. Anyone seriously interested in training is strongly encouraged to look beyond 'what to do' and 'how to do it' and to delve into the areas of why things are done in a particular way.

The authors have been selected because they have considerable practical experience. All have shared, at some time, the same difficulties, frustrations and satisfactions of being involved in training and are now in a position to share with others some helpful and practical guidelines.

All of us are aware of the costs of too much or too little training, not only in financial terms but in terms of the credibility of the trainer. This means that the identification and analysis of training needs must be undertaken thoroughly and systematically. Those who have experienced the 'quick and dirty' approach will readily see the value and the logic of resisting temptation and the exhortations of line managers to produce instant training solutions.

In this book Robyn Peterson clarifies what is meant by identifying and analysing training needs and presents detailed guidelines on how to proceed through a potential jungle of relevant and irrelevant information, of organizational politics and sensitive areas to arrive at a clear understanding of those essential needs upon which training should be based.

ROGER BUCKLEY

Introduction

Training for Real Improvement

It's common in this age of economic upheaval to call for training in all sorts of situations involving performance problems. Sometimes this call makes sense. At other times it makes no sense at all.

Given the large number of educational institutions that now exist, and the often murky distinctions between education and training, inappropriate education or training courses often take place, simply because so many are available. Add to this various kinds of financial incentives that support programmes labelled as training programmes, and training or education can often intrude where it provides no real help. One regrets to say that eagerly-offered training programmes too often lead to more problems than they solve.

This is not to say that educators or trainers are wilfully sinful. It's simply to note that training in business and industry must directly support the goals and objectives of the particular organization in which, or for which, training occurs. Decisions about what training is 'good for industry' made in remote bureaucratic positions are often wrong decisions. The key issue is to make sure that the voice and control of decision makers in various business organizations is strong, clear, precise and well directed.

Trainers engaged in the work of training needs analysis are at the heart of the decision-making process for selecting and designing effective training programmes. The quality of their work in finding real training needs and then ensuring that those training needs are dealt with productively is crucial to quality training in the organization.

In this book, starting in the first chapter, you find key terms laid out along with the structure of the complete training needs analysis process.

The second chapter spells out the importance of your role as a consultant, internal or external. In the third chapter you'll find a thoroughgoing review of performance objectives, including the distinctiveness of their use within the training needs analysis process. In the fourth chapter you find the keys to planning various kinds of training needs activities. The fifth chapter takes you through the actual conduct of the complete training needs analysis activity. The sixth and final chapter delves into a variety of issues connected with actually obtaining the information you need to carry out intelligent training needs analysis work.

Some people object that the full training needs analysis process is too time-consuming or complex. These same people would likely not object to complex and detailed work being done to design a new machine for the production floor. Somehow they can convince themselves that designs meant for human improvement in the workplace can be flung together almost in a state of absent-mindedness. One of the tasks of the training professional is to make sure that the people he or she deals with understand that some of the processes required for ensuring the effectiveness of training demand care, attention to detail, and the proper sorting out and analysis of training needs.

Over the years many people have made valuable contributions to my understanding and work with the training needs analysis process. Sometimes I've been a slow learner. But always I've done my best to incorporate the wisdom they've imparted. I can recognize only a few of them here.

The good advice and challenging thoughts of Bill Patterson, Ray Matsunaga, Brian Mountford, Fred Hill, Patrick Suessmuth, Tony Cunningham, Gord Bonner and Bill Cumberland have served me well over the years. I extend to them particular recognition.

Any errors in writing style or content are my responsibility. I hope you will find precious few.

Dolores Black, Roger Buckley and Robert Jones provided careful and insightful comments and attentive support throughout the production of this book. I give them my warmest thanks.

In this book you will find the information you need to enable you to work professionally with training needs analysis, either for relatively small and localized performance improvement purposes, or for the complete make-over of a large organization. Be flexible in your work, and use this book as a resource to help you meet the different training needs situations as they occur.

1 The Process of Training Needs Analysis

 ▷ SUMMARY ◁

This chapter:
- Sets out the framework for the training needs analysis process. It specifically defines the terms *training need, training needs identification, and analysis of training needs* and relates these to the issue of performance discrepancies.
- Emphasizes the role of the training needs analysis process in ensuring that training is cost effective.
- Deals with the importance of feedback throughout the training needs analysis process, linking it to the concept of continuous organizational improvement.
- Notes the importance of gaining cooperation from people in the actual work group or organization under examination. The question of who should carry out the training needs analysis process in whole and in part is considered.
- Sets out planning and preparation tips to follow prior to engaging in the full-scale training needs analysis process.
- Notes different kinds of causes for human performance problems and cautions against too readily resorting to training.

In Search of Agreement

People within the training community talk often about 'training needs' in pursuing their goals. The term can take on the aura of a talisman for ensuring training will, at least, have surface justification. And training needs are very important. Without establishing them first, training sessions can be ill-conceived and worthless from the point of view of organizational effectiveness.

All might be well and highly efficient if everyone agreed on the definition of training needs and the process of how to identify and analyse them. Unfortunately here's where a lot of problems arise. One person's definition and process might be quite different from another's.

11

Successful training needs analysis demands care, attention to detail, and a determination to search for the performance facts and their implications, rather than simply to justify existing opinions and pressures.

If the term 'training need' is used a little too casually, a lot of undesirable consequences follow. Different people could argue for their own approaches to training or development based on their sincerely-held views that they really 'know' the training needs involved. But, in the absence of an agreed definition, they could be arguing their cases on shaky, even spurious, grounds or even end up arguing about completely different things without realizing it. In this way you get lots of smoke with precious little fire.

Unless the people actually engaged in the full training needs analysis process have a clear idea of what they mean by this important activity, and convey this meaning successfully to others, the results of the most extensive research they conduct into training needs and their significance are likely to be seriously flawed. And the flaws involved could ensure that the results of any programmes that follow will be counter-productive.

Training is Not Necessarily the Answer

Perhaps the number one rule in identifying and analysing training needs is to keep in mind that training is not necessarily the answer to performance problems in the workplace. We're categorically *not* looking for more and more ways in which to give people training courses — although training *may* result from the process.

When training is seized on too quickly as an organizational solution, it can become part of the problem, rather than part of the solution. For this reason, care is needed when dealing with various government-sponsored training incentive programmes. These are truly gift horses whose mouths should be peered into most carefully! The proper training needs perspective provides the magnifying glass to do so.

The whole process of training needs analysis provides a valuable component of any continuing effort to achieve *performance improvement* in the organization. Some practitioners even say that we shouldn't focus on the term *training needs analysis*, we should instead talk about *performance needs analysis*, thus emphasizing the need for training to play a subordinate and supportive role.

Is Training Cost Effective?

Training programmes cost a great deal of money nowadays. A quick cost breakdown for a hypothetical one-week programme for twelve people (Figure 1.1) shows just how much money such a programme might cost in 1992.

This is a conservative estimate, and the specific numbers are going to vary from one organization or work group to the next. Further, it does not take into account out-of-town people travelling to take a course and receiving accommodation.

```
Participant salaries: 12 x 300 =              £3,600.00
Burden (benefits, etc.) 12 x 300 x 29% =       1,044.00
Classroom overheads                              125.00
Materials                                        215.00
Administrative support                           575.00
Replacement employees                            950.00
Instructor (internal)                            293.00
Audio-visual support                              75.00
Transportation                                   120.00
Miscellaneous                                    125.00

Total                                         £7,122.00
```

Figure 1.1 *A cost breakdown for training*

Our estimate, rough as it may be, shows that the cost per employee for this hypothetical training course works out to £593.50. Another way to state this is to say that a person/week of training costs £593.50.

If the training involved does not really meet the needs of the organization concerned, the costs jump enormously. Poorly-conceived or executed training could cost a company or government department hundreds of thousands of pounds; in some cases even millions.

The only way to have truly cost-effective training is to make sure it's based on solid training needs analysis work. This means the conduct of careful research and analysis within the organization *before* any training is actually carried out. And this means, in turn, a solid understanding in theory and in practice of the concept and structure of a training need and of the training needs analysis process.

The Training Needs Analysis Process

Some training practitioners insist that *training needs analysis* (TNA) focuses only on the task of analysing the training needs that have already been identified. Others use the term to cover both the discovery or identification process and the analysis of the needs themselves. Naturally, this leaves room for some confusion. I will do my best here not to add to the inherent confusion that can occur.

For the purposes of this book, when I talk about the 'process' of training needs analysis, I'll consider *training needs identification* as a sub-set of this process. When talking about the 'analysis of training needs', I'll leave out the word *process* as a means of indicating that I'm talking about the analysis of training needs as a specific task dealing *only* with the training needs themselves.

In case confusion is starting to arise, let me rush to include a couple of definitions.

A **training need** is *a need for human performance improvement that can best be met by training of some kind.* For effective analytical use this need must be spelled out in clear, behaviourally-oriented terms. It is vital that training needs, once identified, are written down for easy reference.

Training needs identification is *the process required to detect and specify training needs at the individual or organizational levels.* In effect, this process involves a form of information filtering designed to sort out needs from wants, and then to clarify which of the needs discovered are actually 'training' needs.

The **analysis of training needs** is *the process of examining training needs to determine how best they might actually be met.* In this process such considerations as organizational priorities, costs, resources, and the precise nature of the learning involved come into play. Note here that some training needs might end up not being directly addressed for such reasons as cost, impact limitations, or changing organizational goals.

Put simply, the complete process of training needs analysis involves all those activities and skills necessary to identify and analyse training needs accurately. This means specifying those *gaps or discrepancies* in performance that actually exist between what people are capable of doing now, what they should be doing, and what you want them to do in the future. It also means closely examining the training needs that emerge to determine the best ways of dealing with them given the realities of the people, technology and organization concerned. The more proactive mode required for future needs comes into play when major changes in organizational location, production design or equipment are in the offing.

The complete process has similarities to panning for gold. First you find a likely area for gold deposits. Then you look for and stake out a fast-flowing stream. Next you use a gold pan to slosh your way through a continuing slurry of dirt and pebbles. You next carefully examine your panfuls of slurry to identify the flecks of gold. These you filter out. Finally, you refine the gold dust to produce wafers and bricks of gold. Then you're rich!

The flecks of gold are the training needs. The sloshing and filtering process is the identification process. And the production of wafers or gold bricks is analogous to the final analysis process.

Ideally, organizations should develop a general alertness to performance problems. The training department should certainly encourage this kind of alertness. Symptoms of performance problems may show up in increased levels of absenteeism, time off for illness, grievances, or more numerous accidents. They may also show up in routine boss-subordinate relationships, especially if the bosses concerned engage in 'management by walking around'. Sometimes these problems are glaringly obvious; at other times they're quite subtle.

Sometimes major changes such as organizational re-structuring or technological change will automatically raise performance questions. In this case you might deal with anticipated performance problems or, more positively, performance 'concerns'. The training needs analysis process still applies.

In carrying out the process of training needs analysis, remain sensitive to the organizational climate in which you're working. You have to use a scalpel, not an axe, and it's far better to have key people working with you voluntarily rather than through some means of intimidation, subtle or not so subtle.

When performance concerns exist, the training needs analysis process can swing more fully into play. Line supervisors or managers may engage in this process themselves. They may have trainers to assist them, or turn to trainers to carry the main load of the work required here. A lot will depend on the relative levels of expertise involved and the working relationship that exists between the training group and the rest of the organization.

The diagram shown at Figure 1.2 helps to highlight the key stages involved.

In dealing with the *performance concern*, identifying on-the-job requirements in the form of *performance objectives* is particularly helpful. These types of objectives are behavioural in design, and do much to make the analysis and identification process more precise. It will not always be possible to identify these requirements as performance objectives. Time

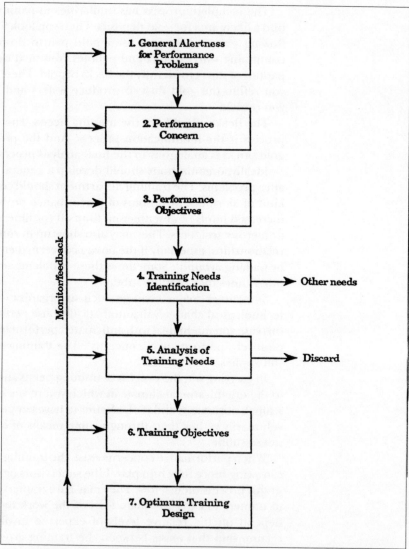

Figure 1.2 *Overview of the training needs analysis process*

and other pressures may not permit. But, if the possibility exists, it should be pursued. Chapter 3 goes into these kinds of objectives in much more detail, and shows how they eventually might become *training objectives*.

At the fourth stage the *training needs* are specifically identified and described. This stage can involve a lot of hard, frustrating work, especially if people have already made up their minds as to what the needs really are. Unfortunately, at this stage a lot of people find themselves attracted to the glitter of fool's gold. The analyst must keep a clear head and search objectively for the real needs, despite misleading information others may uncover or advance. Notice at this fourth stage that you will probably identify needs other than training needs. These needs, which may well be important in themselves, must be looked after through some other process. Figure 1.3 shows what some of these other needs might be and how the organization might deal with them.

Once you discover or identify the training needs, you must analyse them in themselves at the fifth stage and in their relation to all the relevant surrounding factors. They need checking against such factors as practicality, cost, priorities, learning issues involved, organizational plans and so forth. They should also be grouped at this stage to take into account learning hierarchies and logical clustering of needs.

The sixth stage involves translating the training needs into training objectives. These are performance statements similar to performance objectives, but they are designed for use in various types of instructional approaches. In some cases they may come to be called instructional objectives or learning objectives. Further grouping of the original learning needs may occur as you convert them into training objectives.

At the seventh and final stage of the training needs analysis process, selection of the optimum training design becomes essential. This design may include an array of courses including internal corporate ones, courses offered by local polytechnics, or simply self-directed learning programmes. Here everything must finally come together to meet those training needs that have been filtered through the complete training needs analysis process.

In succeeding chapters we will refer back to this model from time to time to help flesh out its detail and to show how and where successive items of information fit.

Feedback/Monitoring

This important aspect of the training needs analysis process needs special featuring. From examining Figure 1.2 you can see that a feedback/monitoring connection exists for each of the stages prior to the seventh. The issue here is that the actual process of designing could well turn up various kinds of anomalies which might reveal further performance concerns or, at least, provide finer adjustments of the concerns or objectives already stated. In writing out some programmed instruction, for instance, what had earlier seemed to be a logical connection in explaining a given chemical process, such as one of the fine points in a particular polymerization process used in the rubber industry, might not turn out quite as logical as first thought. This could well require adjustments of earlier stages to bring all the wording properly into line.

All stages of the training needs analysis process must remain open to further adjustments, although one hopes that such adjustments will be minimal in most cases. Further, if we were to go beyond the seventh stage into the actual provision of training, the feedback/monitoring concept would still apply.

Training analysts and designers need to be cautious about equipping and scripting instructors like so many biological robots to deliver highly structured training programmes offering little or no scope for participant feedback. While structure certainly has a place in training, it can cut off invaluable feedback from employees in different kinds of work settings.

Peter Senge notes in his book *The Fifth Discipline*, "As the world becomes more interconnected and business becomes more complex and dynamic, work must become more 'learningful'." He talks of the 'learning organization', an organization in which workers continue to expand their abilities to learn and cooperate with others. The training needs analysis process can encourage this in a general way by ensuring that feedback channels into the training system remain open, flexible and attentive.

The Japanese management concept of *kaizen* pushes for continuous improvement in the organization. Work systems must never be allowed to become rigid or compartmentalized. Even the most junior worker has a valued input into the whole enterprise. In a sense you can think of this as a micro form of systematic training.

The training needs analysis process can encourage this continuous improvement concept in a productive way. The key is to use it in a thoughtful, probing and flexible way, never allowing it to become a rigid, imposed structure. One must always remember that the solutions of yesterday can become the problems of tomorrow.

The training needs analysis process is not intended only to provide better training programmes, although that is an important consideration. Used effectively, this process becomes a vital component of better management in general. So trainers can become all the more involved as professionals concerned with improving the entire organization, not just practitioners of something called 'training', which can all too readily be viewed as a remote activity unto itself.

Keeping the lines of feedback/monitoring open at all times will automatically help to ensure the continuous inclusion of new information and the refinement of old information. Further, it will help to convince employees throughout the organization that their opinions count and will be considered.

The Importance of Gaining Cooperation

Fully-effective training needs analysis must have the positive cooperation of the top decision makers concerned. Otherwise, it will lack authority and it might be seriously flawed through the provision of inadequate or inaccurate information.

People working at various levels in an organization are in unique positions to know how the company or government department can operate most efficiently and effectively for their work area. They work with the organization's detailed realities every day, so they spot the important little things that almost always escape top management. They also know the kinds of changes or supports most likely to make them fully effective as employees.

The information employees can provide is invaluable. Knowing this fact and exploiting it productively is part of the secret of success for Japanese industry in the past thirty years. The quality circles that are so popular in Japan are one of the best means of bringing out positive information and idea responses from employees. Quality circles themselves often identify real training needs. Here is a crucial ingredient of the true learning organization.

Employee cooperation with and support for training needs analysis is invaluable. But it requires the right kinds of encouragement and the right conditions.

Who Does It?

In some cases the training needs analysis process might be carried out by the organization's own training department. In other cases external consultants might be engaged. Internal people may have the advantage of familiarity with the organization. Sometimes, however, this very familiarity may be a disadvantage, making it harder for them to gain perspective. External people may have objectivity, but they need good access to organizational information. Their very presence could, however, stir up resentments, thereby distorting the information they receive. The question of proceeding on an internal or external basis is one that needs thinking through before the process gets under way.

Depending on the skills of the people involved, much of the analytical work required in the training needs analysis process may be carried out by line people such as supervisors or managers. They receive powerful assistance in doing this if they have access to up-to-date, accurate and performance-oriented job descriptions and position descriptions (often they will have taken part in writing these too).

When the process reaches the stage of analysing the training needs identified, the involvement of experienced training people becomes advisable, because they must clarify the exact training measures needed to obtain the required performance results.

In many cases, using teams will make the most sense for carrying out the training needs analysis process. This will apply particularly when the analysis must cover an entire company or a large department.

The people who make up a good team should provide skills in such areas as expertise in the work areas under examination, knowledge of future organizational developments, understanding of the human resource skills base available, good analytical and communication skills, and a thorough understanding of the training needs analysis process. In addition, at least one member of the team must be a high-ranking officer of the organization. In many cases the chief executive officer would make a natural member.

If an individual or a team lacks sufficient real clout in the organization, the quality of the training needs analysis process will suffer and the ensuing recommendations for performance improvement will too likely be ignored or passed over lightly.

Organizational Benefit

A thorough training needs analysis does much more for an organization or work group than identify the human resource development activities that may or may not be required. It allows the organization or work group to examine itself in a unique way from the point of view of its general organizational effectiveness.

Inadequacies in locations, machines, work designs, safety, health, communications, organizational hierarchies, financial controls, personnel policies, and many other areas will reveal themselves. As Michael Applegarth has pointed out in his book *How to take a Training Audit*, a solid training needs analysis process also forms the core of a good training audit.

A good training needs analysis process provides an *early warning system* for protecting the organization's health. Because a thorough analysis deals with a cross-section of the employees in an organization, it will generally identify most of the issues, problems, and concerns they're observing or experiencing. This is especially the case when confidentiality and fully effective communications are encouraged.

The training needs analysis process can tell an organization much about itself, so its usefulness goes far beyond the requirements of the training department. When thinking about this process, keep in mind its larger role, and avoid thinking of it simply as another training activity. This will help you to keep it in the right perspective. It will also help you to sell it that much more convincingly to top management.

TRAINER'S TIPS

1. Be sure to work out your training needs analysis plan well before you actually start your needs analysis work.
2. Keep in mind always that training is not necessarily the answer to performance problems.
3. Keep the definitions of *training need, training needs identification* and *analysis of training needs* clear and distinct in your mind.
4. Establish and maintain contact with the key decision maker in the organization (this is the person whose decision will make or break the whole process, whether or not he or she actually is the manager or chief executive officer).
5. Remain flexible, and be prepared to revise your training needs analysis plan if key information or important circumstances make this advisable.
6. Work to find the specific performance level the organization now requires in the person or work group concerned.
7. Determine the specific performance level the organization demands for the future — and why.
8. Find out the existing performance level of the person or work group, being sure that this information is soundly-based and doesn't just represent personal opinions.
9. Find out as specifically as possible the opportunities that exist for meeting the individual's or the organization's performance requirements now and in the future.
10. From time to time update the information your key decision maker has about your progress and findings.
11. Always look for objective data to support the information you receive from the people you deal with.
12. Take advantage of the opportunities you will have or can obtain for finding the training needs information you require.
13. Never underestimate the importance of gaining cooperation from the people you deal with in obtaining the information you need.
14. When you have completed your training needs analysis work, prepare a report for your key decision maker detailing your findings and your recommendations for action.

Human Performance Problems

All sorts of human performance problems exist in today's organizations. Not all of them will best be met with training programmes. In fact, it's very likely that *most* of them will best be met by processes or interventions *other* than training.

Such things as inadequate ventilation, noisy surroundings, poor lighting, faulty nutrition, poor communications, bad morale, ineffective management, environmental hazards in general, inadequate equipment, ergonomic inadequacies and poor systems designs can all lead to human performance at work being less than it might be. In some cases *much* less.

Many managers automatically turn to training if they have human performance problems. They think, 'A good training programme will fix these people up.' And, when that doesn't work, they simply look for another training programme thinking, 'I've got to get one that works instead of the last turkey we had.' Yet the real problem may be a systemic one not amenable to training at all.

You can compare prescribing training inappropriately for performance problems to a doctor prescribing different medicines for a patient in need of surgery. Proper diagnosis is essential to proper treatment.

Unfortunately, many trainers reinforce managers in thinking of training as a cure-all for their performance problems. With lots of positive feedback from course participants they provide the 'appearance' of meeting organizational needs effectively. Yet the actual on-the-job results may not bear out this kind of success. At times these results can even become worse, not better. In these cases, training, far from being a cure, becomes a curse.

The diagram shown at Figure 1.3 illustrates the total approach to examining human performance problems in a fully professional fashion. Note that the possible action outcomes can lead to many programmes other than training programmes. So the design stage can link to the design requirements of a number of different possibilities. In the case of identified training needs, this stage would have to encompass the analysis of those needs prior to incorporating them into a training design.

Ill-conceived Training

Suppose a factory has a production problem. Management may look at it and decide that the workers should be producing more. Time-and-motion or work simplification studies may confirm this. A training pro-

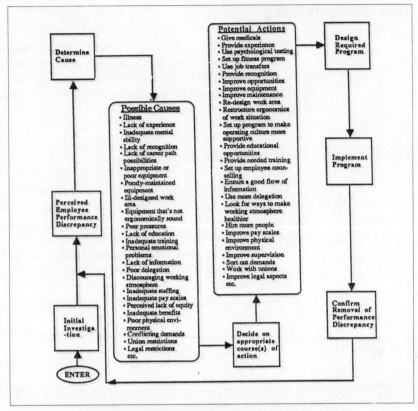

Figure 1.3 *Employee performance analysis chart*

gramme could be set up for the workers to show them how to perform the required tasks properly and efficiently. So far so good.

But what if these workers can already perform the tasks involved in the desired way? Further, what if the real reason for the production problem is the fact that equipment is not being maintained and adjusted properly?

In these circumstances, forcing workers to take training programmes would very likely lead to resentment, and logically so. In effect, they're being told they're inadequate, when they know the real problem lies in the general management of the factory. Here is a clear case where training is likely to prove counter-productive. It's 'training for frustration'.

The only way to make sure human performance problems are addressed objectively and effectively is to ensure training needs are identified and analysed with care and skill. This means, among other things, basing any organizational intervention designed to improve employee performance on well-conceived and well-executed performance analysis.

23

True Quality Training

Training worthy of the name achieves real and tangible results, which will reflect themselves in the improved performance of the employees involved. When training does emerge from a good training needs analysis application, it will be quality training, not something taken off the shelf and forced to fit somehow.

The Successful Training Needs Analysis Process

The successful training needs analysis process brings with it many different rewards. But, as you can see, it's by no means a simple process. It may entail training or educating decision makers about the nature and purpose of the process. This takes time and patience.

The training needs analysis process seldom takes care of itself. And if you or someone else do not do it properly, all sorts of people are only too willing to step in to sell their particular brand of training 'snake oil', claiming for it marvellous powers and considerable fees.

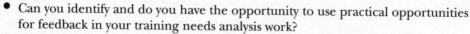

►   QUESTIONS FOR THE ANALYST   ◄

- Can you identify and do you have the opportunity to use practical opportunities for feedback in your training needs analysis work?
- In what ways do you anticipate gaining cooperation from key people?
- Why is it dangerous to engage too readily in using training to solve human performance problems?
- Your boss asks you to make a presentation to a group of senior managers about the training needs analysis process: what are the key things you would emphasize in this presentation?

---

2 Your Role as a Consultant

>   SUMMARY   <

This chapter:
- Notes the ins and outs of your role as a consultant in the training needs analysis process. Some key points to keep in mind to work in the consulting role are set out.
- Gives you key questions and steps to work with at the start of the client relationship.
- Clarifies the differences between an internal and an external consultant.
- Sets out important issues and ideas to consider in sizing up and working most productively with clients. Relates to key points of human motivation in the consultant/client relationship.
- Provides crucial information for managing the fear of change so often provoked by the training needs analysis process.
- Sets out the elements of the client contract you need to establish at the beginning of the training needs analysis process.

Thinking of Yourself as a Consultant

In working on the various aspects of the training needs analysis process, you're most often in the role of a consultant. This applies whether you're on the staff of the organization concerned or you are coming to it from some outside body, such as a consulting firm or some form of institution. It also applies whether you're working on your own or as part of a team. Differences do apply, of course, between internal consultants and external ones. But many of the concerns and approaches are identical.

Fundamentally, the consultant seeks to help key people in the work group or organization identify and face up to the problems affecting them. Some consultants work in a direct, no nonsense way, while others

25

work more subtly and unobtrusively. Because training needs analysis work delves into areas where ready answers are not always available, the more subtle consulting approach will generally work best.

In general, consulting tasks involve these key steps:

1. Making your entrance.
2. Gathering information and analysing that information.
3. Planning options and setting out implementation strategies for those options.
4. Establishing a contract.
5. Bringing about, and following up on, change.

Note how these blend with the section in the previous chapter dealing with the conduct of the training needs analysis process.

Work with the training needs analysis process is work with change — current or anticipated. In this respect the consultant working on training needs may well, in effect, become a change agent for the organization or within the organization.

Approaching the Client Group or Organization

The early stages of the training needs analysis process are vital from the consulting perspective. Here you set the tone and make the working arrangements for everything that follows. If this work is done absent-mindedly or too quickly, you will not obtain good results. So it pays to take care.

When you know or anticipate that you, alone or as part of a group, will be acting as a consultant to a given department or to an entire organization, consider the following questions. In fact, you will probably find it a good idea to jot down some answers to them for yourself on a separate sheet of paper. In the case of groups or teams, everyone might participate. This way, you'll arm yourself all the more effectively for dealing with key people, and for making sure that the early impressions you make are productive ones.

1. How do (or will) people in the client group or organization relate to you?
2. What, if any, is your existing working or hierarchical relationship with them?
3. How, specifically, do you plan to start things off?
4. What do your clients or prospective clients expect from you?

5. To what degree will they be dependent on you?
6. Will they expect to have a continuing link or relationship with you?
7. Are you likely to be perceived by them as an actual change agent, or as an information bureaucrat?
8. Will you have ready access to the people you need to meet or deal with?
9. Will you work directly with the key decision maker or with an intermediary?
10. What kind of commitment has the client or prospective client already made to change?
11. What understanding does the client have at this point about the training needs analysis process?

Your answers to these questions will enable you to work on arranging things most effectively from the beginning. They will lead you to points of clarification and agreement you can work out with your client. This way, in effect, you build your 'working contract'.

Action Steps at the Start

Having just gone over some important points to think about before engaging in active work with your client, next you need need to think about the initial action steps that make sense. Ask yourself or ask your consultant group to go over these questions:

1. Where should action occur (why? and how?)?
2. Who is the key to making it happen (the key decision maker)?
3. What will the work group, department or organization do to make it happen?
4. What will you or your team do to make it happen?
5. When will you start and finish?
6. How will you know when the project is complete?

The answers to these questions will give you a useful initial plan to go on, or at least identify some key questions to ask. Later, in Chapter 4, we'll go into more detail on the planning that should go into the training needs analysis process.

Internal Consultant or External Consultant?

We've noted earlier that you or the team you're part of could work in the consulting role internally or externally. Let us now look at the key differences that are likely to exist for the one as opposed to the other. The following table of comparisons helps to illustrate this:

Internal Consultant	External Consultant
• more time available for the client	• time is at a premium, and must be used sparingly
• part of the organization or work group — so may be part of the problem	• not part of the organization or work group — so has 'distance' and added perspective
• not free to leave the organization or work group when the training needs analysis process is over — must live with the consequences	• leaves the organization or work group after the training needs analysis process is over — removed from the consequences
• generally perceived by the client as less costly to deal with	• often perceived as highly expensive to deal with
• often not seen as an expert	• expert status often conferred
• likely not to have a varied background with different organizations or technologies	• usually brings experience from a wide variety of different organizations and technologies
• usually more confined or structured in job role	• not easily slotted into organizational hierarchy — may be perceived as 'above it all'
• can provide inadequate performance and still survive in organization	• inadequate performance will usually result in termination of services
• may work at a lower hierarchical level	• more readily able to deal with higher-ups in the organization as a whole
• may encounter internal resistance or hostility in the work group or organization	• may be accorded more flexibility as 'unknown quantity'
• closely acquainted with the politics of the organization	• not well acquainted with political realities — may inadvertently blunder here
• knows and works with the language and culture of the organization	• may run into problems by making statements or doing things that convey unintended meanings

Our two listings show that neither one nor the other is automatically 'correct' for a given situation. The people making the decision about using an internal or an external consultant must examine the given training needs analysis situation on its own merits.

In some cases, because of organizational arrangements, internal consultants may have more of the advantages of external consultants. In other cases, the external consultants may have most of the advantages of internal consultants. When such cases exist, they should be factored into the decision-making process here.

In some situations, when groups or teams of consultants are involved, both internal and external consultants may be members. This can combine the virtues of both. Mind you, under ineffective team leadership, it can also bring out the drawbacks of both.

The training needs analysis process is not a fill-in-the-blanks exercise. It involves different decisions to meet different needs. It also involves a continuing sense of flexibility. The internal/external consultant decision is one that needs to be made deliberately for each training needs analysis project.

Your Clients

A vital part of your work in training needs analysis concerns realistically sizing up the clients you're dealing with. This is not necessarily an easy task, but it is a revealing one. We all too easily form impressions about certain kinds of people, then deal with those impressions rather than the actual people themselves.

Some people are obnoxious, especially when they hold a higher position in an organization. But that doesn't mean everyone you encounter fits this negative description. The different people you meet all have their own characteristics. Some are difficult to deal with, while others are ideal.

Approach each client when you first work with him or her on an individual and open-minded basis. This way you free yourself from preconceptions that might be counter-productive to your goals. You're also more likely to find yourself with a cooperative client.

Working Effectively with your Clients

Given that effective work with clients can involve a number of tricky and subtle points, it's important to remain aware of the kinds of things you should or should not do when working with them. The points given here supply you with a comprehensive listing of the actions or behaviours you should engage in when talking or otherwise communicating with your clients.

1. Work to build a relationship of real trust between yourself and the client to promote open information exchange.
2. Ensure that you continually emphasize clear communications.
3. Try to remain open and objective at all times.
4. Work to draw out your client in comfortable and relaxed ways.
5. Resist the temptation to take charge, give directions or advocate certain courses of action (unless such courses of action are very strongly indicated).
6. Look for and pick up on your client's reactions to what you say and do.
7. Be as attentive as possible to everything your client says, concentrating on the items pertinent to the information needs of the situation.
8. Be on the lookout for signs of tension build-up, and work to defuse these when they occur.
9. Note signs of evasion on the part of your client, and take them into account.
10. If your client becomes angry, look for ways of displacing it or defusing it (but work hard to avoid giving in on issues of substance to the training needs analysis process).
11. Avoid becoming flustered, defensive or annoyed when you hear opinions given by other people that seem ridiculous, ill-conceived or hostile.
12. When you feel anger or disagreement arising in yourself, work to control it or channel it effectively.
13. Explain fully those things you anticipate may still be unclear to your client, especially where these involve the technical ins and outs of your analytical work.
14. When your client does or says good things, be sure to offer praise (but don't be ingratiating).

Relating well to your clients is really no mystery. The Golden Rule says it: 'Treat others the way you would have them treat you'; and at all times remain attentive.

> **TRAINER'S TIPS**
>
> 1. Make sure you get things off on the right foot with all your clients when engaged in your training needs analysis work.
> 2. Establish a formal or informal contract with your clients before starting to work on the training needs analysis process. This contract must set out working relationships and expectations of the key parties.
> 3. Work to help your clients understand the ins and outs of the training needs analysis process.
> 4. Always remember the power and value of trust in your client relationships.
> 5. Be prepared at all times to cope with nervousness about or resistance to, change in the work units or organizations you deal with.
> 6. Resist any temptations you may feel to become dictatorial or autocratic. At the same time, present yourself and your information clearly and confidently.
> 7. Work to relate most effectively to the needs and reactions of your clients.
> 8. Involve key people in the work group or organization as much as possible in carrying out the training needs analysis process.

Tips on Motivation

In many ways, in your work as a consultant, you're concerned with motivating others. In this connection, it's useful to keep in mind some of the key points involved with human motivation in any situation. Most of these are based on the excellent work done by Frederick Herzberg and Abraham Maslow over the years.

It's not at all unknown for people to know how to do a particular job and yet not actually do it, or at least not do it up to the mark. Why? Often it's a question of the motivational factors; or contingencies that are at work.

Are people really rewarded for performing well? Do they feel it's worth their while to do a good job? Or do they feel overloaded and unappreciated? Perhaps they feel their colleagues will dislike them for doing a good job. All these things and more can influence the degree to which a person actually does or doesn't do what she or he is capable of doing.

If you disregard the motivation factor at any stage of the training needs analysis process, you run the serious risk of producing training for frustration.

The workings of human motivation are not simple, although we can describe them in fairly simple terms. We respond to things going on around us in a number of different ways all at the same time. Sometimes we respond very quickly without lasting impact. At other times we respond deeply and can remain motivated for a very long time.

The following issues can play a significant role in helping to promote motivation of the deeper kind. Conversely, their absence can lead to demotivation.

- the presence for individual employees of positive personal responsibility
- the availability of interesting challenges
- clear evidence to the employee of personal achievement
- open recognition of one's efforts
- a genuine sense of excitement in one's work and the surrounding activities
- a feeling of being productively involved
- a genuine sense of personal growth as time passes
- the sense that what one is doing is truly worthwhile

In searching for the presence of healthy levels of motivation, bear in mind the significance of these points. Work to find them from the point of view of the people you're concerned about. If some or all of these points seem to be absent, look for ways of including them in the work of the people you're dealing with. This will give you added information for use in dealing effectively with all the different kinds of needs the full training needs analysis process will bring out.

Managing the Fear of Change

Many people fear change. It conjures up the unknown for them. Will they have to learn something new or difficult? Will they lose status or respect? Will someone else replace them? Will their set behaviour patterns become useless? What will happen to their nice, safe, and predictable world?

When you're involved with carrying out the training needs analysis process, you're automatically associated with some sort of change in people's minds. For this reason, it's important to think about how people react to change, and what you can do to help them see change as a productive occurrence in their lives.

Everyone fears change from time to time. It can catch us at an awkward time. It can cause us extra work, just when we thought we'd done enough. It can irritate us by disrupting or removing a given routine or programme right at the point when we thought it was starting to work well.

Sometimes change seems worthwhile after the event, but at others it seems like a waste of time. We learn that change does not necessarily bring good things in its wake. Sometimes it can be the beginning of a long decline in a department or an entire organization.

Less experienced employees tend to view the prospect of change with less fear than those with longer memories. This can come about simply from the fact that they've not been around long enough to go through periods of change that brought poor or disastrous results. In their eyes change offers novelty, excitement, motivation.

Some 'old hands' can become so disenchanted with the very idea of change that they become stubborn and fixed in their ways. They can become fanatical in their resistance to change, even to the point of sabotaging its occurrence.

We know, or should know, that change is necessary for organizational health. It aids in removing toxic elements, such as outdated procedures or items of equipment, and allows the introduction of new ways of doing things along with up-to-date technology. In fact, with today's world economy change is essential. The corporate motto nowadays could well be, *change or perish.*

If you suspect that the people you're working with might suffer from the fear of change, be sure to take this into account in the way you deal with them. Pay special attention to those issues that could cause fear or rejection in the minds of others.

Here are some general points to bear in mind when seeking to deal with the fear of change:

1. The bigger the prospective change, the more essential the need to give people *relevant information* from time to time before you propose the change. This allows them gradually to adjust mentally to what's coming, thereby lessening the surprise factor.
2. Identify the *opportunities* your ideas or information will open up from the point of view of the people you're dealing with.
3. Relate any changes you propose to existing and successful examples (being sure these are credible to your audience).
4. Show people how their existing knowledge and skills fit within the proposed change framework.
5. Under no circumstances give the people you're trying to persuade the impression they're out of date or lacking in education or expertise (even if true!).
6. Be careful about emphasizing the qualifications of yourself or others as related to the proposed change, especially if these appear to outclass those of the people you're talking to.

7. If possible, relate your proposed changes to past statements or actions by the people you're dealing with which logically relate to or support the proposal.
8. Look for ways to involve people before, during, and after the change or changes being proposed, and ensure that they understand the nature of the *contribution* they can make.
9. Always be very clear and positive about the reasons why the proposed action or plan will prove better than the system or set-up that exists already, being sure to spell out these reasons in terms other people will understand and appreciate.
10. At all times be sensitive to and try to provide for the security and status needs of the people you're working with, being as specific about meeting these needs as you can.

The human fear of change can often be irrational. Nevertheless, its consequences are real. In any organizational or institutional setting you ignore them at your own peril.

Establishing a Contract with Your Clients

Your clients, as your decision makers, are the keys to the success of your training needs analysis work. You can't emphasize this point too much. To deal with them successfully demands care in planning and paying attention to the details.

The more important the issues you're confronting, the more important is the question of active cooperation and support from your clients. In working this out, you're establishing a contract. This contract can be implicit or explicit. Whichever it is, it must cover these vital areas:

1. A clear setting out of the responsibilities of all those associated with the training needs analysis process.
2. Objectives for each segment of the process.
3. Clear monitoring/feedback points for the process, including key criteria for assessing progress.
4. Time frames for each step or segment of the training needs analysis process.
5. Rewards and results to expect from the process.

In the next two chapters we will look at the specific ways you can describe and set out these important contract items. For now, consider the importance of your client contract to your own success and that of your client.

The Productive Relationship

When you develop a good relationship with a client, you've gained a critically important plus in carrying out the training needs analysis process. Unless you develop this kind of relationship, your work is likely to prove inadequate or worthless.

Clients don't have to cooperate with you. They may benefit if you do a good job. On the other hand, they may also benefit if you do a poor job. From the point of view of organizational politics, it's sometimes handy to have someone else to blame for poor results. And your client could pick you for that unfortunate role.

You might say the client sometimes wins from making you lose. But you're unlikely to win by making your client lose.

You need to work always on the win/win basis. Keep reminding your client in various ways of what's in it for her or him. This improves your chances of keeping her or him on your side. And try, at all costs, to avoid doing those things you know your client will find difficult or impossible to support or endure. These are your 'no go' areas, and you need to know them well.

The productive relationship is possible to build. But it takes time, effort, and patience. And you or your team as a whole are responsible for providing these essential ingredients.

▶   QUESTIONS FOR THE ANALYST

- Do you see yourself as an internal consultant or an external consultant? What are the implications here for your training needs analysis work?
- Think of the clients you must deal with. What are the specific things you can do to help motivate them?
- To what degree do you believe the fear of change may exist within the company?
- What steps have you taken in the past to set up contracts with your clients?
- Are the clients you deal with always completely honest with you about the details and problems involved in their various work areas?

3 The Performance Perspective

▷   SUMMARY   ◁

This chapter:
- Provides the behavioural focus needed for all aspects of the training needs analysis process.
- Notes the influence of behaviourists on the corporate world.
- Defines the behavioural objective.
- Defines the performance objective as a form of behavioural objective.
- Sets out the concept and usefulness of performance sets.
- Links performance objectives and sets to training objectives and training modules.

A Fundamental Concern

One concern is fundamental to the complete training needs analysis process. That is to ensure that you retain a good perspective on performance throughout. This applies to the way you set out performance standards, examine and clarify performance problems, and analyse training needs.

The Behavioural Focus

The behavioural focus in examining human activities essentially says that you must look at what people do or don't do, not what they profess or claim to do. This focus is crucial. It provides a means of clarifying issues in objective detail. It also provides the basis for developing full-scale technologies of learning.

The people you deal with in organizations will probably tend to stress attitudes or idea issues, rather than actual behaviours. While attitudes and ideas are important in their own right, it's human behaviours that actually get things done. Productivity is a function of excellent on-the-job behaviours, not nice thoughts or pleasant dreams, although the latter play an important role in supporting and helping to develop the behaviours desired.

The Behavioural Perspective

The term 'behaviour' is used in a variety of ways. Mothers use it when referring to the habits and activities of their children, especially when these involve misbehaviour. In everyday life and at work we may use it in a general way to describe how someone is acting (eg 'Joe's behaving a little strangely lately.'). In brief, we may use it simply as a term to describe the way someone conducts him or herself.

These general uses for the term are valid in themselves. But you can also use this term in an applied sense, much the way psychologists do (particularly those described as behavioural psychologists). In this sense a behaviour is a specific and observable act by a given individual.

J.P. Chaplin in his *Dictionary of Psychology* gives the following definitions of behaviour:

1. Any response(s) made by an organism;
2. Specifically, parts of a total response pattern;
3. An act or activity;
4. A movement or complex of movements.

We're not concerned with turning ourselves into psychologists here, amateur or professional. But these definitions help sharpen our perspectives for examining performance — for the essence of performance is behaviour.

If you pick up your pen from your desk, for instance, you're engaged in a behaviour, that of *picking up your pen*. When you write with it, you're engaged in another behaviour, that of *writing*. When you place your pen back down on the table you engage in yet another behaviour. In fact, the process of writing a memo can be broken down into a set of such behaviours (and laying out this kind of set can be a useful thing to do at times, especially when concerned with analysing training needs).

Most of us have heard of the Russian physiologist Pavlov and the experiments he carried out on his dogs before and after the First World War. From his work psychologists developed important theories about conditioning and the process of behaviour reinforcement. Among these theories were those of B.F. Skinner, concerning what he called *operant conditioning*.

Operant conditioning stresses the concept of observing an organism until it starts moving in the desired direction or behaving in the desired way. The moment this initial 'correct' activity takes place, it is rewarded. Early rewards are the greatest. They gradually diminish with each succeeding correct activity (following a reinforcement schedule) until either small rewards or no rewards at all are needed, because the organism has incorporated the desired behaviour into its fundamental behavioural repertoire.

The behaviourists have had a profound impact on the corporate world through their work on performance incentives, performance improvement, positive reinforcement, and various employee motivation plans. All require the careful setting out and use of behavioural objectives to specify desired behaviours (sometimes referred to as terminal behaviours). These behaviours become the specific targets towards which people are directed with varying organizational interventions from incentive programmes to training programmes.

Focusing on human behaviours in this highly-specific fashion yields many useful insights into what people do and why they do it. For this reason a behavioural approach to examining human performance in diverse settings gives us a very powerful tool to work with. Like all powerful tools, however, the behavioural approach requires some care in application.

People are not merely machines or biological robots. They have feelings (affective activity) and they think (cognitive activity). While more radical psychologists insist we're nothing but behavioural organisms, most agree that we have features beyond the strictly behavioural. So when we use a behavioural approach for examining on-the-job performance, we must also keep in mind its limitations.

Behavioural Objectives

These are objectives for people's behaviours. They are not 'wish' statements or 'activity' statements, nor are they the same as 'aims'. In his book *How to Take a Training Audit*, Michael Applegarth sets out a useful distinction between on-the-job aims and objectives as follows:

Aim   The general direction and purpose for which something exists.

Objective The specific event to be achieved while travelling in a known direction.

The diagram at Figure 3.1 helps to illustrate this further. The 'aim' arrow in this diagram could also be describing an activity. In effect, it's a question of means versus ends.

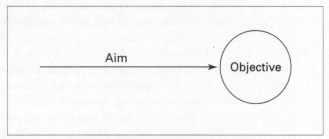

Figure 3.1 *Aim versus objective*

A good behavioural objective tells us:

1. What the person will do (in concrete terms);
2. What standard of performance will apply (timing and quality);
3. When he or she will do it.

A sample of such a statement would read:

"The artist will, when presented with a palette of paints of different colours, select the correct colours to mix 'spring green'. He or she will do this within ten seconds."

The 'what' here is the selection of paints. The 'standard of performance' is the correct colours within ten seconds. And the 'when' connects directly to the time of presentation.

A behavioural objective is an action-oriented statement. It focuses on real things happening. It must stand up to testing in the actual work environment. So it cannot be theoretical or simply express a wish. Further, it must be something that the employee can clearly understand and verify.

Some people are uncomfortable with this way of expressing human achievements. They find it somehow dehumanizing. But it should be seen and used only as a tool, not as a device for turning people into biological robots.

Behavioural objectives set out a highly-specific language useful for describing and planning human activities in a variety of settings. It's a language well worth using.

Performance Objectives

Partly to avoid confusion with other areas, such as various types of institutions for providing people with therapeutic care, the use of a term other than *behavioural objective* for training needs purposes is helpful. The term *performance objective* is one such term.

A performance objective is a specifically-stated requirement for a person performing a particular task. It lays out the what, how, and when of task performance as well as the standards required. Here is an example of what a performance objective might look like:

> *The personnel trainee will use his/her desktop computer to access the personnel procedures data base for specific references to ensure information accuracy when replying on the telephone to employee inquiries about job classifications. On average, each such reference will take no longer than one minute and will be conducted in a polite and positive manner.*

We've identified the what: *'... access the personnel procedures data base ... employee inquiries about job classifications';* the how: *'... use his/her desktop computer';* the when: *'... when replying on the telephone...';* and the standard: *'On average, each such reference will take no longer than one minute and will be conducted in a polite and positive manner.'*

Here's another example:

> *The employee will safely change any burned-out fuse in the fuse box of the G23 press within fifteen seconds using the correct procedure as laid out in the manufacturer's product manual. The employee will perform this task upon determining that the previous fuse is burned out.*

In this example, the changing of the fuse is clearly identified as the task required. The standard of performance is laid out with the specified timing and reference to the manufacturer's procedure. The 'when' in this case is the moment the fuse is discovered to be the problem with this machine.

Performance objectives take time to produce. They may need to be discussed and rewritten a number of times before they really describe the performance involved. Small but important nuances might be left out at first. It may be necessary to observe someone actually doing the job to get the right feel for the words needed. Sometimes it's even a good idea to do the job yourself to make sure you're familiar with all its fine points. Written notes of all these fine points are essential. Sometimes sketches, photographs, videotapes or audiotapes also help in analysing the task or job under examination.

Well-conceived and well-written performance objectives become the key ingredients or building blocks for examining human performance issues in as specific and detailed a manner as practical. Skill in identifying them is essential for objective training needs analysis.

Here's another example of a performance objective:

> *The employee will re-calibrate the Mark IV radiometer by hand to an accuracy level sufficient to measure radioactivity levels within a tolerance of*

0.1 rem (roentgens per minute). This re-calibration will normally take less than thirty seconds.

Once again you can identify the what, how, when, and standards required.

Given enough time and sufficient access to critical information, you can theoretically break down any job into its constituent performance objectives. This kind of breakdown makes sense for more repetitive or behaviourally-oriented jobs. It falters when dealing with more conceptually-oriented jobs, or those requiring significant decision-making activities, especially when these activities concern new or novel issues. Nevertheless, the skill of identifying performance objectives remains essential.

Performance objectives play an important role in conducting a full-scale job analysis to determine the specific skill and knowledge requirements of a given job and all its component parts. In effect, they describe the foundation structure for the job or its core, including all or almost all the skills required. The knowledge requirements may not always lend themselves to being worded as performance objectives. But they should be 'pushed' to see how far they can be moved in that direction.

Suppose someone says a given job demands that its incumbent have 'a good knowledge of first aid'. You have to ask more questions. What does a good knowledge mean? Or what is a person *doing* when he or she demonstrates a good knowledge of first aid. This line of questioning could eventually bring you to the point of finding that the job-holder must demonstrate:

- the use of pressure to control or stop bleeding
- proficiency in caring for a patient suffering from shock
- the correct way to handle a patient suspected of having suffered spinal injury
- treatment of a victim suffering from acid burns
- use of the Heimlich manoeuvre for dealing with a choking victim
- treatment of a poisoning victim
- application of cardio-pulmonary resuscitation
- correct handling of a victim of an epileptic seizure

This kind of performance-probing soon lets you see that what initially might have been described as knowledge actually involves quite specific skills. And these lend themselves to being set out as performance objectives.

Our list of first aid skill requirements does not yet form a performance objective or a set of performance objectives. But it's well on the way. A little more work on the standards of performance and the time to use them, and a good performance objective or set of performance objectives will emerge.

The key to using performance objectives well is to use them for the right reasons and with appropriate areas of concern. You can't use them willy-nilly to describe everything. But if you target them well and use them with precision, they're invaluable.

Exercising Balance

Most of the things we do at work are not matters of individual performance objectives identified at the minutest level of observed activity. In describing the performance of writing, for instance, it probably wouldn't serve much useful purpose to break it down into its constituent behaviours this way:

1. Picks up the pencil from the desk using thumb and forefinger of right hand, grasping at a position set back approximately 30 millimetres from the point of the pencil, ensuring that the length of the pencil lies on the hand;
2. Places point of pencil on paper exerting sufficient pressure to cause the lead to mark the paper;
3. Moves the pencil up and down and back and forth on the paper to produce letters that create words and recognizable messages;
4. Having completed the task of writing a particular message, puts the pencil down on the desk in a flat position and removes the grip of thumb and forefinger.

In dealing with human beings at work, we assume a reasonable existing skills base or repertoire for activities such as writing or talking. So the useful setting out of performance objectives works with identifying performance at a level suitable to the reasonably-assumed existing skills level of the people involved. In other words, you might not really have to specify how a person uses an ordinary screwdriver (although you might, at times, want to specify limits such as using only insulated screwdrivers for electrical work, or refraining from using screwdrivers as levers).

In some cases, of course, more detailed performance objectives or sets of objectives have a place. If you're managing dolphins or apes, for instance, you might need these kinds of sets or individual objectives, because the skills base won't be there. Similarly, if we need to communicate some day with beings from another planet, we'd be well-advised to think specifically and very basically about the things we do ourselves or ask of them.

Some human beings may need more detailed performance objectives set out for them. People from different cultural groups or people with lower levels of education might well need more detail. Deciding on the most appropriate level at which to write performance objectives requires knowledge of the subject population, experience, and sometimes a little trial and error.

Some psychologists use the term *perceptual trace* when referring to the way we automatically tend to cluster our actions and move smoothly from one to the next in carrying out a given task or job. Human beings usually organize their thinking and acting automatically this way. We do things in a flow of connected actions, rather than in a series of specific tiny acts. You might also term this an *action pattern or action template.*

Whatever term you use, you will find it allows you to focus conveniently on a performance, such as setting a table, without necessarily having to break it down into all the little behavioural steps involved.

The key is to work with a reasonable sense of balance or proportion in deciding which tasks in a given job or work area need to be set out in performance objective terms, and which might conveniently be left to the realm of perceptual pattern or trace.

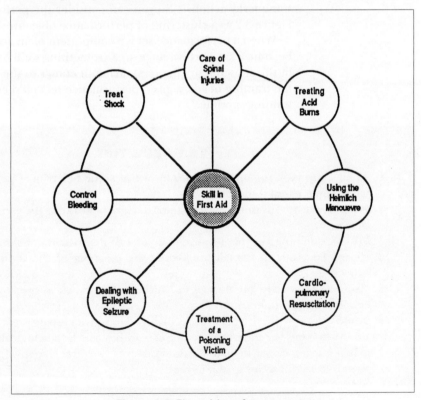

Figure 3.2 *First aid performance set*

Performance Sets

When you do need more complex structures for setting out performance objectives, the *performance set* comes into the picture.

Consider our earlier example of first aid skills. You might view this as shown in Figure 3.2.

In effect, this displays the performance set for skill in first aid as a form of molecule, with the subsidiary performance objectives taking on the role of electrons orbiting around the first aid nucleus.

In this case it makes sense to consider each of the 'electrons' as a performance objective in its own right, because you can readily view each as a perceptual trace area. In examining the Heimlich manoeuvre, for instance, you can visualize that a person should carry this out in a general, flowing fashion, not in a series of specific jerky little behaviours, although those little behaviours will be incorporated into the total performance flow. (Mind you, in actual performance, this manoeuvre may well involve some jerky actions!) So you can consider the performance set given in Figure 3.2 as a clustering of performance objectives.

When a performance set is a component of an actual job, it is likely to become a key performance area (something we'll be talking about more in the subsequent chapters). When it comes to the process of analysing the training needs, a given performance set could emerge as a complete training module.

TRAINER'S TIPS

1. At all times look for opportunities to examine the behaviours people engage in when going about their jobs.
2. Keep an eye out for the reward systems that are at work for the various people you deal with.
3. When examining any job, be sure that you can describe it in behavioural terms.
4. Always be ready to explain to people the meaning of the term 'performance objective'.
5. Exercise balance in the degree to which you may seek to break jobs down into smaller tasks or operations.
6. When working with the behaviours involved in a given job or work area, always be on the lookout for the performance sets within which they logically might fit.
7. When moving closer to actual training, be ready to translate performance objectives into useful training objectives.

Translating to Training Objectives

In the training needs analysis process, some performance objectives will lend themselves to being converted directly into training objectives. Put in its simplest form, this conversion process occurs as shown in the diagram at Figure 3.3. Notice that this diagram is a portion of Figure 1.2 in Chapter 1 *(Overview of the training needs analysis process).*

The training needs identification activity will screen out those performance objectives that can best be met by other means such as work experience, job aids, equipment adjustments, ergonomic changes, and the like.

The identified training needs require further analysis to determine how they might best be approached from a training point of view. This can entail thinking about issues such as training equipment, training locations, and instructors. In some cases this analysing process may show that it is just not feasible or practical to meet some identified training

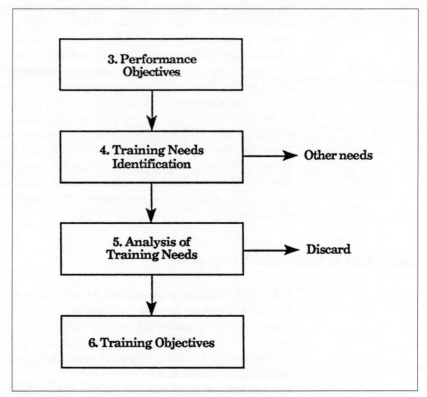

Figure 3.3   *Transition from performance objective to training objective*

needs through formal training of some kind. The reasons for this can vary from excessive costs to organizational change. Such training needs are then discarded.

Discarded training needs are not necessarily forgotten. Individual employees, for instance, may decide to meet them on their own through part-time courses and the like. In other cases discarded training needs may come back into formal consideration at a later time as a result of another training needs process conducted for another part of the organization. The important thing is to realize that identified training needs will not, in themselves, necessarily justify setting up formal training programmes.

Sometimes performance objectives will emerge from this process unchanged in their wording, so a performance objective may simply be re-labelled as a training objective. This could particularly be the case if the optimum training approach is on-the-job training or some form of simulation. In other cases rewording will occur to reflect such training design issues as lesson planning, classroom layout, learning time and the like.

Notice, by the way, that when the time comes to write out a training objective, you're concerned with what the learner will do, when, and to what standards: the same basic requirements as for a performance objective, but converted to focus on a learner instead of an employee, and to focus on the training location as opposed to the work location (remembering that some forms of training can take place in the work location).

In some cases, depending on the intricacies involved, the training objective may have to be much more detailed than the performance objective. This will be a necessity to meet good learning requirements. Doing something, learning how to do something, and teaching someone how to do something are three distinct areas of activity, and these differences may well be reflected in the exact wording of a training objective.

Individual or Corporate Perspective

Just as the training needs analysis process can apply at the individual or corporate level, so too can performance objectives. You might, for instance, need to examine jobs across a company because of technological change, or because of corporate reorganization (including retrenching or take-overs). Similarly, you might need to examine one person's skills repertoire in performance terms, including the use of practical demonstration tests, to determine his or her degree of suitability for a given or planned position.

The use of performance objectives is by no means restricted to the process of training needs analysis. Performance objectives are fundamental building blocks for a range of human resource development and planning activities. They crystallize thinking and force clarity on generalized statements. They help decision makers to better understand the performance issues about which they need to make their decisions. In short, they help to cast a lot of light into the dark corners of human resource development.

Different people in the organization might become involved in writing out performance objectives. It is not necessarily the special preserve of trainers or the training department. Normally, however, one would expect trainers to be involved in some fashion, either as the key analysts or as consultants to those responsible for the various phases that occur within the training needs analysis process.

The more widespread the use of performance objectives for various purposes within an organization, the easier the job of full-scale training needs analysis. You will more readily find well structured and well stated job analyses. The task of identifying training needs in the first place becomes easier. And the analysis of those training needs will become more straightforward.

Continuing Perspective

As noted at the beginning of this chapter you need to retain a good perspective on performance throughout the full training needs analysis process. This perspective informs your thinking and sharpens your analytical work.

You can do much to build and sustain this perspective by keeping it in mind in everyday occurrences on and off the job. When you go the supermarket, for instance, analyse the work of the cashier at the checkout. What performance objectives do you see in his or her work? (As well as sharpening your analytical skills, this would give you something to think about other than the fact that the queue is taking forever to move along! Similarly, you can analyse the work of the waiter at your favourite restaurant (thereby, at times, helping to identify flaws in the service).

The performance objectives perspective will help you in all aspects of the training needs analysis process. It will also serve you well in many other areas. It is well worth developing.

▶ QUESTIONS FOR THE ANALYST ◀

- What specific examples have you encountered in your career of problems arising from the differences between what people actually 'do' in a work setting as opposed to what they're supposed to 'know'?
- Think of a job description you've worked with recently. Was it phrased in behavioural terms or in more general work-related statements?
- Think of a key performance area with which you have a lot of experience. Can you set out a performance set for that area?
- Do the training objectives you work with relate readily and observably to actual performance objectives?
- In the future do you anticipate working mainly at the individual level or the corporate level in your training needs analysis work?

4 Planning Your Training Needs Analysis Work

▷ SUMMARY ◁

This chapter:
- Outlines with examples the use of the action appraisal in early planning stages.
- Provides a layout example.
- Shows how important factors can be sorted using the factors chart.
- Links in the use of the options comparison matrix.
- Makes the link to the training needs analysis process plan.
- Sets out, and explains with examples, the key parts of the training needs analysis process plan.
- Includes the basic layout of a PERT chart.

Think Things Through

From all that's been said up to this point, it's obvious that you need a lot of good, precise information in working through the complete training needs analysis process. This kind of information will not normally fall into place either conveniently or quickly. Indeed, if it does, you should examine it all the more closely to ensure that unwitting prejudices are not coming into play inadvertently. What to do? The key thing is to sit down and think things through carefully before taking action. In other words, plan your work well beforehand.

Preliminary Plan of Action

In setting out your preliminary plan you can borrow from the field of good management practice. The model outlined here is the *action appraisal,* an adaptation of the *military appreciation* format. The military appreciation was not developed for civilian management or training needs analysis purposes, but was originally meant to help military officers develop sound plans for deploying their troops and equipment in actual combat. The essentials of this same planning approach have now come to be widely used in management practice. Most problem-solving approaches, too, essentially use this approach. The adaptation presented here provides you with a means of taking a careful look at a proposed training needs analysis activity to identify your best course of action.

If someone calls you in to examine a performance problem area of some kind, you can use this model to set out all the important details and realities of a situation in a methodical way. This helps prevent rash or inappropriate action, and goes far towards ensuring that the plan you decide on is well-conceived and well-directed.

An action appraisal gives you a good base for a training needs analysis plan. It also lets you know if the full-scale training needs analysis process should be brought into play. So it's worth some effort. The main elements of a good action appraisal follow.

Action objective

This is the result or outcome you want from your appraisal work. In dealing with training needs analysis it identifies what you need to achieve in your analysis.

This statement:

1. Contains clear, end-result language that identifies what your analysis will produce.
2. Includes the date for completion of the analysis.

An example of this type of objective:

This analysis project will determine the training needs within the despatching office for improving the operational effectiveness of that work group as a whole. Completion date is June 9, 1993.

Notice that in this example the outcome specified will identify the training needs. It will not include the analysis of those needs to determine the ways in which they might be met. This objective statement may later be adjusted to give you an objective for setting in motion the full-scale training needs analysis process.

In effect, you have here an early decision point. Should you go for the full-scale process at this point? Or should you concentrate just on identifying the needs? In the latter case you could worry about how to meet those needs most effectively at a later stage. Indeed, you need to identify the needs in the first place before you can analyse them in detail.

On the other hand, the performance problem issue involved here may have such importance that the full-scale training needs analysis process is called for at this stage. Senior managers can, in effect, make this decision for you, so you should word your action objective accordingly.

In examining the statement of the action objective given here, note the similarity of concept to laying out a good performance objective. This is a further illustration of the point made in the previous chapter about why it pays to develop a performance perspective in your thinking about results related to human resource development in general. The same thought process will serve you well in many different applications.

Factors involved

These include all factors having a direct bearing on achieving your objective. You can subdivide them into *helpers* or *blockers*, depending on whether they'll help you achieve your objective or hinder you.

Factors could include *support from the key decision maker* (a helper), *a generous amount of time* (a helper), *union hostility* (a blocker), and so on. All impinge one way or another on your likely success.

The factors chart shown at Figure 4.1 helps you set out logically all the helper and blocker factors. List all the factors on a blank sheet of paper first. Then decide which are helpers and which are blockers.

Enter each blocker or helper on the factors chart on the appropriate side of the vertical interface line. Draw each factor as a horizontal arrow against the interface line. The length of each arrow corresponds to its relative impact on your training needs analysis objective. Arbitrarily limit your impact weights using a scale of 4. The strongest factors receive weights of 4 pro or con, while the weakest factors receive weights of 1. Weights in between register as either 2s or 3s on the plus or minus side.

The factors chart gives you a clear means of identifying and sorting out the factors against each other. In some cases you may find 'factor splits'. These could occur, for instance, where you have some members of a group for you and some against. You might have to depict these pro and con groups as two different factors, one a helper, the other a blocker.

Depict factor splits on the factors chart by showing them immediately opposite each other. Factor splits seldom occur evenly across the interface line.

FACTORS CHART

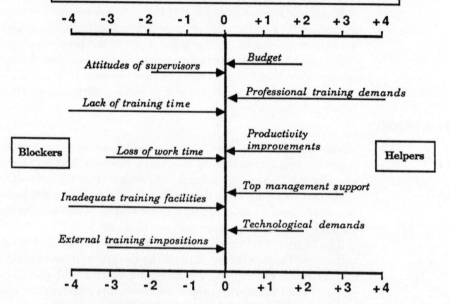

Training Needs Analysis Objective
To determine the training needs for accountants working in the Claims Section of the Central Administration Office by Aug 14, 1991.

Helpers to Highlight
Budget, professional training demands, productivity improvements, top management support, technological demands

Blockers to address:
Attitudes of supervisors, lack of training time, loss of work time, inadequate training facilities, external training impositions

Figure 4.1 *The factors chart*

At times you'll find it convenient to set up a factors chart on a large display area such as a whiteboard or flip chart. This works well for team or work group approaches.

You may find that you need changes on your factors chart as time passes. New factors may come into play, for instance, or existing factors could change. Our illustrated chart is by no means intended as a complete depiction of the factors that might be involved. It might make sense, for instance, to work on the factors of demographics, availability of trainers and so on. The intention here is simply to illustrate how you can use the chart.

Retain your factors chart for later training needs analysis work. You'll find it invaluable in preparing reports and presentations of different types.

Options available

These are the action options you believe you should consider for reaching your training needs analysis objective, taking into account all the relevant factors you have identified. These could include:

1. Completely identifying the training needs involved by conducting interviews at all levels with key personnel, having questionnaires filled out by all employees affected, using on-the-job observations, making comparisons with other organizations, and using an experimental work model.
2. Conducting a partial analysis to include only interviews with key managers and a review of job descriptions.
3. Conducting only a preliminary analysis, with a complete one possibly to follow at a later date.

In coming up with your list of options, be open and creative. Avoid killing good ideas prematurely. Now is not the time to make your judgments. These come later. Note, too, that your options might take into account methods not mentioned specifically here.

As far as possible, lay out your options in summary form. This is part of a preliminary action plan, and you don't want to overcome your options with details. You can get into these later when you flesh out your plan more fully.

Ideally, consider no more than *five* options in your appraisal. It's possible that one of the options you should consider is that of not conducting a training needs analysis at all! (The blockers might be too overwhelming.)

Planned course of action

Select the one option most likely to work given all the factors involved. Establish the likely impact of each factor (blockers and helpers) on each of your options. The option that survives this factor comparison process in the best shape is the one you want.

The options comparison matrix shown at Figure 4.2 gives you a useful tool for comparing the options you've identified in terms of the factors you set out earlier. For convenience, you might set out all the helpers at one end of the row for factors and the blockers at the other. The use of different colours could help set out this split.

To fit the space available, you might need shortened versions of your options and factors. You might also need to extend the number of columns for situations involving a larger number of factors.

When you've got all your options and factors entered, you're ready to

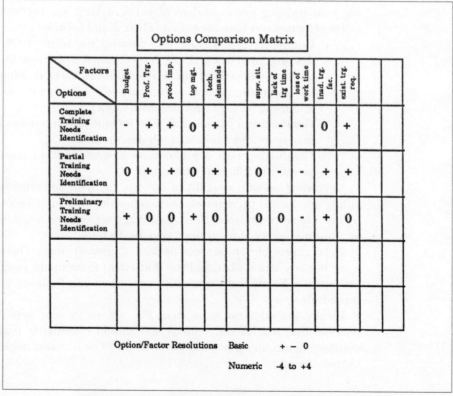

Figure 4.2 *The options comparison matrix — basic*

compare them with each other. You are seeking a *resolution score* for each tor against each option.

Underneath the options comparison matrix are the option/factor resolution entries. One is basic, the other is numeric. Using the basic option/factor resolution method you enter a '+', '-', or '0', depending on whether you think the option concerned will benefit from that factor or suffer from it. If the factor concerned will have no impact on the option one way or another, mark in a '0'.

Note that in our example at Figure 4.2 the entries have been written in using the basic resolution method for our three action options against each of the factors in turn. The factors correspond to those set out in the factors chart at Figure 4.1. The positive factors have been set out in Figure 4.1 first, with the negative ones set out to the right of the blank column. This order is by no means necessary, nor is the blank column. Use this matrix structure in the way that best makes sense to you.

Options Comparison Matrix

Factors \ Options	Budget	Prof. Trg.	prod. imp.	lop mgt.	tech. demands		supv. att.	lack of trg time	loss of work time	inad. trg. fac.	exist. trg. req.		
Complete Training Needs Identification	-2	+3	+4	0	+2		-1	-2	-4	0	+3		
Partial Training Needs Identification	0	+2	+2	0	+3		0	-3	-3	+4	+1		
Preliminary Training Needs Identification	+1	0	0	+4	0		0	0	-3	+2	0		

Option/Factor Resolutions   Basic   + − 0

Numeric   -4 to +4

Figure 4.3 *The options comparison matrix — numeric*

The numbers set out on this sample matrix in Figure 4.2 are arbitrary, because this is a hypothetical case. Add up each of the rows to produce algebraic sums for each action option. In the first case, for the complete training needs identification option, the sum is 0 (four 'plus' entries and four 'minus' entries). The next option, partial training needs identification, gives us a sum of 3. The third and final action option produces a sum of 2. At this preliminary stage of comparing the options, the middle option has the best score.

At this point we've scored each option against each factor using the basic resolution approach as noted at the bottom of the chart. We could go on, next, to use the numeric resolution approach, which is to say we attach numbers to the option/factor cell that better reflect the weight of that particular option/factor combination.

Our diagram at Figure 4.3 illustrates the use of the numeric resolution

Options Comparison Matrix

Factors / Options	Budget	Prof. Trg.	prod. imp.	top mgt.	tech. demands		supv. alt.	lack of trg time	loss of work time	inad. trg. fac.	exist. trg. req.		
Complete Training Needs Identification	-4	+12	+8	0	+4		-2	-8	-12	0	+9		
Partial Training Needs Identification	0	+8	+4	0	+6		0	-12	-9	+16	+3		
Preliminary Training Needs Identification	+2	0	0	+12	0		0	0	-9	+8	0		

Option/Factor Resolutions   Basic   + – 0

Numeric   -4 to +4

Figure 4.4 *The options comparison matrix — factor/numeric*

approach. Adding up each row now gives us an expanded view of the weights of each option against each factor. This expansion usually makes it easier to spot the options that best stand out. Once again, of course, the numbers selected are arbitrary ones used for illustration.

A glance back at our factors chart at Figure 4.1 shows that we attached numbers to the factors in drawing the lengths of their arrows. These numbers, however, were produced concerning the training needs analysis objective we started out with originally.

For further refinement, we could set out an options comparison matrix that integrated the weights of our options against the factors with the relative weights of each of those factors. We can use the numbers set out at Figure 4.3 for this by multiplying them by the factor weight numbers shown at Figure 4.1 In doing this, we disregard the sign of the factor at Figure 4.1, using only the sign showing at Figure 4.3. The result is displayed at Figure 4.4.

This factor/numeric approach enables us to take into account the weights of each of the factors as well as the weights of the options against those factors, thereby giving us more discriminating results. It involves a bit of work, but it's work that can justify itself in the longer run.

In using the options comparison matrix, you are using what is formally known as a *subjective-linear* decision-making model. This model gives you one of the highest quality decision devices you can employ. The word 'subjective' comes into play because we recognize that a certain amount of subjectivity is inevitable in deciding which factors are important, and then assigning weights to them.

The only decision-making model with a higher quality is the *objective-linear* decision-making model. This latter model is built using factors that have proved impact and weight, either through experience or practical experiment. The latter model forms an important part of the structuring of good *expert systems* making use of computer technology.

For your purposes, you can sharpen the subjective-linear options comparison approach by doing the best you can to ensure that you've identified all the factors at work and given them reasonable weight attributes. The more you involve other people in the organization in this identification and weighting work and make use of actual performance data, the better. Such involvement can move your decision-making process in the direction of a full-scale objective-linear comparison approach.

Other organizational factors will, of course, come into play to influence how far you can go in determining factors and weights. Here the question basically becomes, 'How much will this really be worth to my company?' If it seems likely to prove cost effective, the search for solid factors and justifiable weights for those factors could take over two years.

In such a case you would probably be dealing with a training need area that had crucial significance for the health and effectiveness of the organization in the years ahead.

In less momentous cases, your work on the factors and their weight impacts would possibly come down to a matter of weeks or months. In a few cases, depending on the quality of the data available, you might conduct this work in a matter of days, but this is not likely to happen very often.

Whatever the time and effort investment involved, the option that works best against all the factors becomes your planned course of action. And your planned course of action serves as the basis for your *training needs analysis process plan*.

Advantages of the Action Appraisal

At first the action appraisal approach outlined here for setting out your preliminary training needs analysis plan might seem cumbersome or unduly complicated. With practice, however, it becomes easier to use, so it will end up as second nature to you. Remember too, it's up to you when and if you use it. There will be cases where it makes sense to start right in to the training needs analysis plan in full.

The action appraisal process can apply to various stages of the training needs analysis process, as well as to tasks removed from training needs analysis altogether. The idea is to use it where and when it makes sense to you.

You can remove each of the three tools illustrated as part of the action appraisal process for use on their own elsewhere. Any time you need to consider the impact and significance of clashing factors in a situation, you can use the factors chart. The options comparison matrix or a modification of it will apply to those situations where you need to make a choice between, or among, different options.

Good thinking is essential to good analytical work. By developing your skill in using the action appraisal approach, or parts of it, you improve the incisiveness and effectiveness of your thinking, particularly when dealing with complicated issues and problems.

The Training Needs Analysis Process Plan

This is your plan for carrying out your complete analysis of the training needs of a given organization or work group. It flows logically from a good action appraisal, and you detail all the critical aspects of the planned analysis that are important to a useful and complete analysis. The plan format given in Figure 4.5 provides a good outline.

The initial information concerning the *organization/work group*, the *location*, and the *date(s)* is important orienting and logging information. Concentrate on one organization or work group at a time. For the record, set down the location or locations involved as well as the date or dates. All the information you gather will lend itself to future reference for different kinds of training and development work.

The *authorizing person* is your key decision maker. This is the person who gives you the authority to conduct the training needs analysis in the first place, thus providing you with your terms of reference. Often these terms of reference are best written out to avoid confusion or dispute later on. This authority is essential in giving you the kind of access you need to do a thorough and fully competent job. The authorizing person is also the person you report to at the completion of your analysis.

TRAINING NEEDS ANALYSIS PROCESS PLAN
Organization/work group
Location(s)
Date(s)
Authorizing person(s)
Training Needs Analysis Objective
Target Population
Key Performance Area(s)
Requirements for Conduct of Analysis
Required Performance Objectives
Performance Discrepancies
Apparent Reasons for Performance Discrepancies
Identified Training Needs
Analysis of Training Needs
Training Objectives
Recommended Training Design

Figure 4.5 *The training needs analysis process plan*

The training needs analysis objective is the statement of what you want to determine from your training analysis, and when. It could take the following form:

> *This analysis project will identify and analyse the training needs within the despatching office for improving the operational effectiveness of that work group as a whole. Completion date is June 5, 1993.*

Notice the difference between the wording of this objective and the wording of the objective we used in dealing with the preliminary plan of action. That objective focused on *identifying* needs. This one *identifies* and *analyses* them, so it's pointing at the complete training needs analysis process.

Add details to your training needs analysis objective as they make sense. The more concrete you make it in terms of the questions *who?* and *what?* the better.

The *target population* is that specific group or number of people whose performance you will examine. Carrying on from the training needs analysis objective we just used, you might identify the target population in that case as:

> *All personnel whose job descriptions indicate they have a significant role to play in despatching all types of road traffic at the despatching office in Clearhaven.*

The *key performance area* is an area or sphere of activity included as part of a job, or identified as an important performance objective set within a given area of work responsibility. In job descriptions and the like it might be called a *key duty*. In our continuing example this might be stated as:

> *The continuing provision of accurate and timely communications to the managers and drivers of all types of vehicles being despatched. This includes communications given in person, in writing, over the telephone, and by two-way radio. These communications include all messages related to the effective and safe despatching of road vehicles. They may also include such communications as, in the opinion of the training analyst, seem to have significant impact on communications directly related to despatching.*

Notice in this case we've built in a little manoeuvring room for the person conducting the analysis. This is often a wise precaution, because you are never quite certain beforehand what your research will turn up and the amount of work you will face when it comes to analysing the training needs you uncover. The same point applies to writing out the training needs analysis objective and the description of the target population. This may give you some additional points to negotiate with your key decision maker. You simply have to marshal your arguments to justify their inclusion.

For convenience, you may decide to shorten the wording for the key performance area concerned. Taking our example, for instance, you might refer to it as *'Communicating with the drivers and managers of all vehicles being despatched'*. You'll need to do this in filling out the 'Job Performance Audit Form' which will be dealt with in detail in the next chapter.

Requirements for Conduct of Analysis outlines those personnel, physical,

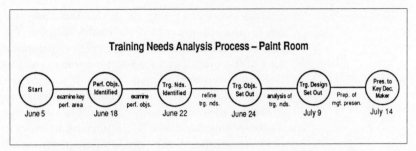

Figure 4.6 *PERT Chart – training needs analysis process*

material and time resources needed by the analyst or analysts. You're making a job estimate here. Because you'll be working in the dark, at least to some extent, you need to be careful in the way you lay out this section of your plan. You must ensure you have sufficient resources for a credible and useful job.

Consider your physical requirements. Will you use your own office or will you need one specially-assigned? Will there be just yourself or will you have a colleague or two and, perhaps, support staff? Will you use an outside consultant?

What about such basics as a telephone or access to a computer? What access will you have to manual files or data bases? How will you store your information as you gather it? What arrangements do you need for security?

You need a time estimate for your analysis. A (PERT chart helps with this. A hypothetical chart is shown at Figure 4.6. PERT, by the way, stands for 'programme evaluation review technique'. It was developed and used extensively to help the American nuclear submarine building programme in the 1950s.)

Two key terms in PERT are 'event' and 'activity'. Circles depict the events, while horizontal lines drawn between the circles show the activities needed to reach those events. In complicated cases the PERT chart may be expanded to include parallel tracks of activities and events. These will depict 'side activities' that must be completed along with other activities. In all cases the chart starts with one event and ends with one event.

Some people also use the term 'critical path' for this kind of layout. In practice you will find some variations on the theme with this charting process, but the outline set out in our diagram is perfectly usable.

The PERT or critical path process applies anywhere you have to set out the details of some kind of project and predict completion times. PERT will help, too, if you have several smaller and parallel training needs analysis processes going on under the umbrella of a general training needs analysis process. This could happen, for instance, if separate processes are conducted for different departments within a company as part of the overall process for the company as a whole.

Even a simple time plan laying out your estimated timings for all the events that have to occur for completing your analysis will work. Be sure to lay out all your time requirements honestly and accurately and don't, whatever you do, 'force fit' important activities into unreal amounts of time. Remember, you're the key person who will be held responsible for the quality of the analysis.

In examining the details given in Figure 4.6, don't become too fixed on the exact dates or the exact events shown. The idea is to note down those events and activities that make sense for your own training needs analysis purposes.

At times, in laying out your requirements, you may need a cost estimate. In producing this estimate, adopt the same rigour as you apply to your time plan. In fact, you may be able to use your time plan or PERT chart as a basis for setting out your costs. Be honest and accurate. And don't forget to include the costs of other people or physical and material resources.

The area of *required performance objectives* is likely to be the trickiest one of all to work with. Most organizations and work groups don't have well-laid-out listings of performance objectives for any job position within their organization chart. If you're lucky they will have job descriptions or position descriptions to work with. But these are usually out of date, and may represent nothing better than 'wish lists' for employee performance.

Earlier we looked at good performance objectives and the kind of information they must contain. In developing your list of performance objectives for a particular training analysis you may have to use a number of sources. These could include the supervisors involved, existing position or job descriptions, members of the target population themselves, and actual on-the-job observation.

In explaining this part of your plan to the key decision maker or the authorizing person, you have to show how you intend to establish the required performance objectives. The more this person understands what this entails, the more she or he can help. You could give some examples of good performance objectives, so she or he will know more precisely what you'll be looking for.

Once you get to *performance discrepancies* you're really getting near the heart of the matter. In explaining these, point out that your intention is not to lay blame or point the finger. You want the facts to speak for themselves. Either there are shortfalls in performance or not. No amount of fancy footwork gets around this point.

You might consider an analogy with a chemical refinery. You've put raw data through a series of filtering and reaction processes to produce refined information. This information, like refined oil, has its own qualities. And these must be dealt with as they stand without any fudging of data.

If the performance discrepancies you identify in your analysis are compromised in any way, particularly for the demands of organizational politics, then your training analysis loses validity and starts to move in the direction of becoming someone's wish list or opinion list.

In considering the performance discrepancies, you may find yourself examining the skills available in a local recruitment area. This could well apply, for instance, if you're dealing with a new factory or institution. A discrepancy in this kind of situation might then exist between the skills of prospective employees and the skills shown in the required performance objectives. In some cases this kind of discrepancy might eventually lead a company to set up training for new recruits to bring them up to the performance requirements before they actually start work.

In detailing this part of your plan to the key decision maker, remain alert to any suggestions or concrete offers of help he or she can give you. You want this person on your side. So listen!

While the performance discrepancies themselves take a lot of effort to identify, and may not receive organizational recognition immediately, *the apparent reasons for the performance discrepancies* can prove even trickier to deal with. You'll have to be specific in pin-pointing the reasons for the discrepancies, as far as possible, in clear, cause-effect terms.

Some reasons are relatively 'safe' to identify. Training and education, for instance, are often simple kinds of issues. Managers know everyone needs more training or education at some point (although, curiously enough, they often exempt themselves from this piece of wisdom). Problems in communication can generally be 'sold' to decision makers. But most other areas that might impinge on performance effectiveness can very quickly involve issues of organizational politics. Large and small hurricanes of power can blow all over the place to obscure issues and distort facts.

In laying out the apparent reasons for performance discrepancies, choose your wording carefully. You have to understand the different 'power centres' you're dealing with so you can enlist support where possible, while avoiding stepping on critical toes — and all this without compromising the objective validity of your work! A fine balancing act indeed. This is a situation where the factors chart or the options comparison matrix might prove useful.

Even though training is seen as a worthy intervention in most organizations, the *specific training needs* you propose may or may not meet with quick acceptance. Decision makers have a funny habit of anticipating the kind of training people need, so they won't necessarily relate effectively to your listing right away. Once again, you find yourself dealing with the realities of organizational politics. Something to bear in mind here is that you're trying to make it easy for your decision maker to say, 'yes'. You have to help him or her see things your way. Never expect the needs you lay out to be 'self evident'.

TRAINER'S TIPS

1. **Be prepared to work through the action appraisal process with others whenever it seems to make sense for planning purposes.**
2. **Set out a factors chart (even a very simple one) whenever you face making a decision involving definite pros and cons.**
3. **Make up an options comparison matrix whenever you face the task of selecting among three or more options in a given situation.**
4. **Use the key performance areas (KPAs) concept to give you a quick grasp of a given job or work area. This will help organize your thinking, and hold off the detailed work of setting out performance objectives until you're ready.**
5. **Practise using the PERT chart process for helping you with planning in areas other than the training needs analysis process.**
6. **When setting out performance discrepancies, always seek to identify them in positive terms, without any hint of negative or finger-pointing connotations.**
7. **When setting out your training needs analysis process plan, always be ready to explain how this process will prove helpful to the productivity of the organization concerned.**

The *analysis of training needs* as noted in Chapter 1 is the process of examining training needs to determine how best they might actually be met. Here you basically focus on the kinds of learning needed, and the kinds of training or education needed to supply this learning. The next chapter goes into this in more detail.

The *training objectives* emerge naturally from the analysis of training needs. As noted in Chapter 3, these can be worded identically to performance objectives. In most cases, however, they're not likely to be identical, simply because they take into account the requirements of the training situation as opposed to the work situation. Depending on how many of these objectives you have, they may need to be arranged in logical groupings or hierarchies, showing their interconnections for particular skill and knowledge issues. In some cases these groupings or hierarchies might be complete performance sets.

The *recommended training design* section of your training needs analysis plan is a very important section. Here you come right to the heart of the matter. How will the decision makers resolve the performance discrepancies that lend themselves to the training solution?

Your recommended training design will outline the *how, why, when, where* and *what* of the training you propose. This may include details of different courses, interconnected courses, courses external to the organization and so forth. Some of these courses may already exist in some form, and simply have to be organized. Others may need to be designed from scratch. Formal educational institutions of various kinds may be involved or cooperation with other companies may appear logical.

The permutations and combinations of this last stage of the training needs analysis process plan are many. Their structure and interconnection depend heavily on the quality of the analysis performed on the identified training needs.

In going over your complete plan with the key decision maker, always be honest about the kinds of issues that will inevitably crop up in conducting the training needs analysis process properly. Obtain his or her support for dealing with these issues in the most effective way possible. The more delegated authority you have, the better. The people you're dealing with must understand that the various aspects of the training needs analysis process require serious attention and commitment.

A well-conceived and well-explained plan goes far towards ensuring success in your training needs analysis work. It gives you clear guide posts for your identification and analysis activities. It also serves to help flesh out your contract with your key decision maker or authorizing person.

Preparation

Preparation is everything in the training needs analysis process. Your plan, gaining the full cooperation of the decision makers involved, and making sure you've got yourself and your materials together beforehand, are vital.

When you plunge into the day-to-day task of identification and analysis, your time will be swallowed up by details and the people you're working with. Sound and detailed preparation in all its aspects is crucial.

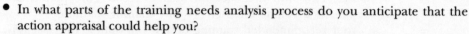

▶   QUESTIONS FOR THE ANALYST   ◀

- In what parts of the training needs analysis process do you anticipate that the action appraisal could help you?
- How would you set up a factors chart for examining a given performance area in your company?
- What decision-making uses can you think of for the options comparison matrix?
- In your own work group or organization, would you be able to apply the full training needs analysis process plan for tackling performance problems? If so, how?
- How would you lay out a basic PERT chart for completing one of your own projects?

5 Conducting Your Analysis

▷   SUMMARY   ◁

This chapter:
- Points out the need for attentiveness to the details in dealing with an organization for the first time using the training needs analysis process. The importance of client commitment to the process is highlighted, and the details for setting up a base of operations and making coordination links are set out.
- Outlines the steps to go through in conducting the training needs analysis process. Making up a task outline is explained.
- Provides complete explanation for identifying performance discrepancies. The use of the Job Performance Audit Form is illustrated with detailed examples. Describing and setting out performance discrepancies is explained.
- Sets out the key points of difference between education and training and shows how these affect the training needs analysis process.
- Clearly describes the analysis of training needs and the importance of this stage of the process.
- Outlines the description and role of training objectives and their relation to the final recommended training design.
- Spells out the need and provides details for inclusion in the training needs analysis report. The requirement for different types of presentations about the results of the training needs analysis process is noted.

Your First Encounter

You begin your assessment of any organization the moment you have your first contact with it. This is why many companies take great care in the selection and placement of their switchboard receptionists. They know the importance of first impressions.

67

When you first encounter any work group or organization, size it up in as dispassionate a manner as possible. Don't let yourself be overwhelmed or underwhelmed by the apparent friendliness or coldness of your reception. Work on looking beyond the immediate impressions. With practice, you'll pick up an amazing array of information.

You may say that these pointers might be useful for an external consultant, but what about the internal consultant? Developing the same habits of assessment applies. The work group or department you enter may not be entirely new to you. But, if you're engaged in the work of training needs analysis, it is new in the sense that you need to approach it with a fresh perspective. And the reception accorded you will reflect the awareness of others that you'll be examining and making determinations about areas of performance. So the reception could be cool or a little different from normal. On the other hand, it might be welcoming and suited to the return of an old friend. Either way you're picking up valuable information.

Bear in mind too that you may be part of a team at work. For convenience I'll use single pronoun references when talking about the analyst here. But these points could also apply to a team working together on the training needs analysis process.

If you're going in to a given location to conduct training needs analysis (either as an external consultant or an internal consultant), ask yourself the following questions as you take things in:

1. Am I generally being treated as a serious professional or as some sort of 'interfering body'? (In the case of groups or departments I've dealt with before, can I detect subtle shifts in their treatment of me?)
2. Do the people I see have an air of calm competence about them?
3. Does the equipment used seem to be in well-maintained running order?
4. How solid a grasp does my contact person have of the work group, department or organization's purpose and relative success? (Am I hearing propaganda or intelligent assessment?)
5. Is my contact person trying to rush me or to keep me from seeing or hearing certain things?
6. What evidence is brought out initially of possible employee performance problems?
7. What information exists, and can I have access to, about earlier performance interventions (training courses, motivation surveys, etc.) and their outcomes?
8. What kinds of comments and help am I likely to receive from line people at various authority levels?

9. Do I see signs of open or covert opposition to any kind of probing into performance effectiveness?
10. Am I likely to have the opportunity to carry out a full and credible training needs analysis process?

Write down your answers to these questions. At the very least, do this after your first encounter meeting. This preliminary information could be vital to the planning and conduct of your analysis. It will also alert you as to how valid your final analysis of the department or organization may turn out to be.

In the early stages your comments to the work group, department or organization must be kept constrained. You don't want to promise too many things too soon. There's a critical difference between engaging in the training needs analysis process and selling a training programme, potential or actual. You need to make it clear to all concerned that your analytical work may lead to some training, but then again it might not. So, in strictest theory, you could end up in a position where the analysis of training needs becomes unnecessary because none exist. Even if this is the case, the training needs analysis process will most likely have proved worthwhile.

When you're satisfied that your contact person is serious about improving employee performance and is in a position to make and implement definite decisions about this performance, start moving towards specifics. (Note here that in a few cases your contact person could be your key decision maker for the whole training needs analysis process.)

Now, the most important issue is to gain definite commitment from the organization or work group to do the work necessary for the planning and implementation of the training needs analysis process. You must be absolutely clear at this point about who your key decision maker is. You can't deal effectively one or two steps removed from the real authority.

If you're an external consultant, shortly after you've left the premises of an organization or work group for the first time, record all your impressions and information about that organization in some form of writing. Attach relevant business cards, organization charts, brochures, and the like. This preliminary research report could prove important to you later on.

If you're an internal consultant, act in much the same way as the external consultant after you've had your first contact with the department or work group concerned. This applies even if you've worked with that department or work group before. To keep yourself in the best analytical frame of mind, you need to remind yourself now and then of the importance of maintaining a certain objective 'distance' from the people you're dealing with. This does not, of course, mean behaving in an unfriendly way towards them, but does mean being cautious about letting social familiarity cloud your judgement.

Even if you don't receive a real commitment towards carrying out the training needs analysis process during your first contact visit, writing out a preliminary research report still makes sense. Months or even years later the work group, department or organization may suddenly 'come round'. This could particularly be the case for the internal consultant. If that happens, your report will give you a good starting point for preparing yourself for another visit.

Your Operating Base

Sometimes the organization or work group you're working with will make an office available to you. This can apply even for an internal consultant, particularly if the organization is large and far-flung. This helps, provided it does not put you too much into the main flow of daily work activities. You need time to think and plan. You also need secure storage facilities for the information you gather.

If the host organization doesn't provide you with this kind of base, set one up elsewhere, bearing in mind your continuing need for some degree of seclusion and a good degree of security. At times you may be able to set up a hotel room to serve this purpose.

Liaison/Coordination

We've noted the need to identify and deal effectively with the decision maker for the training needs analysis process. But you must also take into account possible requirements for continuing liaison and coordination. You may need contact with people at various levels of supervision in the company. Or you might want to have a 'subject expert' available to you, such as a highly-experienced tradesman. Depending on the scale of the entire project, you may need several such people in different locations. Further, there may be some spin-off activities they can engage in for you to contribute to your knowledge about the training needs issues involved. Think through these potential requirements and provide for them.

Other training or educational groups or organizations might be involved from the outset. Just from your general overview of the situation at the start, you might realize that your local polytechnic will play a future role in providing the training needed, so you could want a good liaison person there. Perhaps a training board is, or should be, involved. Again, liaison is needed.

In the case of educational or training bodies, you might want to request a delay in a new education or training programme to allow for revision pending the outcome of your training needs analysis work. In such instances, you'll need to prepare good presentations to justify your request.

In thinking about and planning for your liaison and coordination needs, the action appraisal technique brought out in the previous chapter will help you. Similarly, you may find the options comparison chart useful for sorting out your thinking.

The Steps Involved

The exact steps you go through in carrying out your analytical work may vary from one situation or organization to the next. In general, however, these steps will look something like this:

1. Conduct a *general appraisal* of the entire work group, department or organization. This helps you to get the feel of things, to paint the 'big picture'. (There may be an appropriate role here for producing an action appraisal.)
2. List all the immediately identified training needs (eg new technology may automatically single out such needs).
3. Identify the actual and potential human and non-human sources of information (internal and external) for effectively probing into training needs. (These could include specific managers, supervisors or foremen, employees themselves, people engaged in similar work in other organizations, employee training records, job descriptions, position descriptions, technical manuals, employee appraisals, accident reports, performance data, down time records, and the like — anything at all that might help your research.)
4. Draw up lists of the key performance areas of all the employees whose work you'll be examining.
5. Determine the methods you will use in carrying out the training needs analysis process (interviews, meetings, documents review, use of questionnaires, observation, external visits or consultations, etc.)
6. Develop a list or lists of performance objectives for the key performance areas. (Note here that you're quite likely to identify clusters or sets of performance objectives in doing this, as illustrated in Chapter 3.)
7. Note those key performance areas and performance objectives that

don't measure up in actual results (drawing on the information available to you at the third step).

8. Lay out the specific performance discrepancies for the employees and key performance areas and performance objectives concerned. (Note that the wording may remain the same.)

9. Identify the probable causes of the performance discrepancies (including your evidence for identifying them as causes).

10. Draw up an initial list of training needs from the causes identified, including setting them out as training objectives. (Note here that this setting-out process will probably involve logical groupings of the training objectives.)

11. Analyse the training needs, setting out such things as the types of learning involved, the ideal learning locations, and the likely instructional methods required.

12. If practical and possible, lay out the options available for meeting other kinds of performance needs (another potential use for the options comparison matrix).

13. Specify the organizational consequences of the performance discrepancies (why, in specific terms, are these important to us?).

14. When training is called for, draw up a general training design, at least in outline form. This design should identify the different courses required, the lengths of these courses, the sources of instructors, the evaluation processes to be used, and the locations.

15. Prepare a report detailing the work carried out in the training needs analysis process, including the objective, the actual work groups or departments involved, the methods used, the resources (human and non-human) employed, the findings, and the training recommendations. Additional points might be detailed here depending on the exact terms of reference agreed earlier with the key decision maker.

Laying out the steps this way helps to illustrate how major a job the full training needs analysis process can really be. It also serves to underscore the importance of solid preparation and organizational support.

Notice too that this list of activities is fully consistent with the model *Overview of the training needs analysis process*, laid out in Figure 1.2.

The Phenomenon of 'Functional Fixedness'

Functional fixedness is a brain problem and we're all subject to its influence and impact. This phenomenon describes how we can become fixed in our minds about the uses to which we may put a particular item or tool.

In various parts of Texas, people eat rattlesnake steak. They declare it delicious barbecued. Asked to contemplate such food, people from other parts of the world might well gag. Why?

People in a boat that's filled with too much water work at bailing out with their hands because they have no bailing bucket. They wear large hats which could be filled with water, yet do not use them for this purpose. Why?

In frigid climates people have frozen to death in their cars when they experienced mechanical failure or became stuck in deep snow. This occurred despite the fact that they still had upholstery, fuel in the petrol tank, and a functional electric cigarette lighter. In other words, they had all the necessities to keep themselves warm until they were rescued. Yet they did not use these items. Why?

In all these cases, and others like them, the probable culprit was functional fixedness. People identify a given item as having a particular purpose, and then simply don't think of it as serving a purpose other than the one they associate with it.

In performance terms you might also think of 'operational fixedness' where people work in a certain way because they've become fixed in that way, or they seek to solve problems in a given way because that's simply the way they go about solving problems.

Functional or operational fixedness can become most detrimental to carrying out good training needs analysis, because people at certain levels in the hierarchy may insist on applying given approaches to certain situations, quite apart from whether those approaches are really appropriate.

Develop your sense of alertness to this phenomenon so that you can spot it when it occurs. Be sure to realize that you too can be fully subject to this kind of fixedness. You have to work at forcing yourself to look at things from all sorts of perspectives as often as possible. In that way you'll develop the ability to see things that others cannot see.

The use of specific steps and tools in carrying out training needs analysis work will help you to avoid the pitfalls awaiting those who are unaware. Trust your methodology and apply it rigorously.

The Task Outline

Sometimes you may need to produce a task outline for a particular key performance area (KPA). This breaks down the KPA into its task components. Here's an example of what one of these might look like for a key performance area within the job of a window cleaner. The KPA here is 'washing the windows on an office building':

1. Assemble required equipment;
2. Inspect equipment for damage or excessive wear;
3. Check roof winch to ensure it's in proper working order;
4. Attach rope platform to roof winch;
5. Buckle on safety harness gear;
6. Attach bucket of water and window cleaner to platform;
7. Position body securely on platform;
8. Carefully lower bucket of water over the edge of the building, allowing the platform gently to take up its weight;
9. Grasp winch control lever firmly in one hand;
10. Position feet on edge of roof, ensuring rope is firmly under control;
11. Ease off the roof, slowly walking feet down the side of the building using the control lever to pay out rope as needed;
12. Stop at first window, placing feet on its lower ledge and setting control lever brake;
13. Attach safety line to building;
14. Wash window with careful, slow motions using sponge side of window cleaner;
15. Brush away excess water using rubber side of window cleaner;
16. Unhook safety line and proceed to next window down;
17. Continue sequence of moving to windows and washing them until last window on lowest floor has been washed;
18. Lower self slowly to street level;
19. Return to roof by lift and raise equipment using winch.

Task outlines might vary a little in their wording for the same key performance area going from one work group, department or organization to another. Differences in technical terms or names of equipment may arise. Different terms might be used for the task outline itself. The important thing here is the setting out of the performance information in clear, step-by-step terms.

In helping you carry out the complete training needs analysis process, task outlines can be invaluable. They give you the skeleton on which you can build such performance standards information as timings, how the task is done, the quality requirements, the tool or instrument requirements, and so on.

In setting out this list of tasks you might find it useful to note the *performance criteria* for each task either at the end of your list, or in a column to the right of the tasks. This heading would allow you to set out clearly all the criteria that apply, arranging them against the tasks to which they apply. In doing this you could find it helpful to consult the relevant technical manual as well as the key people connected with the job or key performance area.

Later on you will use the items in the task outline to produce performance objectives for the key performance area concerned. Note that these objectives may or may not coincide with the tasks on a one-to-one basis. In some cases one performance objective might be worded to capture three or more of the identified tasks. Conversely, one task might break down into two or more performance objectives.

When you come to the point of analysing the training needs, you may find that the task outline helps you to develop skills analysis outlines to more exactly pinpoint learning requirements. It is detailed work, but it makes a big difference to the precision and effectiveness of the complete training needs analysis process.

Identifying Performance Discrepancies

The *job performance audit* is the mechanism for identifying and spelling out performance discrepancies. We've seen in the previous chapter that a performance discrepancy exists when there's a difference between what the organization expects in performance and what it actually receives. As far as possible, this kind of discrepancy must be stated in clear, performance-oriented terms. Using the job performance audit you can actually state it as a specific performance objective.

The diagram shown at Figure 5.1 illustrates the portion of the total training needs analysis process (introduced in Chapter 1) covered by the

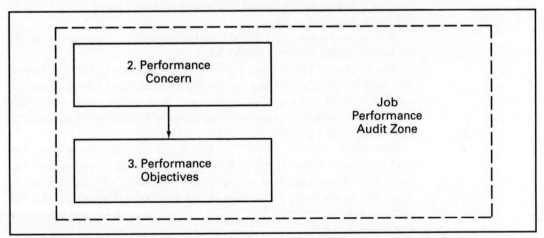

Figure 5.1 *The job performance audit zone of the training needs analysis process*

job performance audit. This audit sets the stage for direct training needs identification.

Those performance objectives identified in the job performance audit as not being met in actual job practice become the statements of performance discrepancy. You might then lay out these discrepancy statements suitably clustered to represent the key performance areas or tasks they derived from in the job being audited.

You can later analyse the performance discrepancy statements to determine those which might best be met through some form of training intervention.

Whatever the details of the plan you finally develop, you must focus as fully as possible on what people *do* as opposed to what they say when conducting a job performance audit. Use apparent attitudes and related comments to guide you towards the actual behaviours relevant to your analysis.

The *Job Performance Audit Form* shown on page 77 (Figure 5.2) is an invaluable tool for the process of identifying and noting down the key issues involved in conducting a good analysis. It is set up to lay out the performance objectives for one task within the key performance area of 'Start-up inspection', which forms one part of the job of 'Parcel Courier'.

The *key performance area* is essentially as laid out in your Training Analysis Process Plan, although, as we noted earlier, you may wish to refer to it by a convenient title form (partly to allow you to fit its name into the space on the form). In some cases the key performance area may be synonymous with the job title for a particular organizational position. In most cases it should conform more to a specific area or focus of work activities. Sometimes the word 'job' refers to a total piece of work involving more than one person.

Notice, by the way, that this key performance area corresponds to the performance set brought out in Chapter 3.

The *Outline of Tasks* column provides for your entry of all the important tasks involved in carrying out the job being audited. Given up-to-date job descriptions, you can obtain a listing of these tasks in short order. You may have to check them against actual on-the-job requirements as seen by all the important parties.

This audit example shows that laying out the tasks for a given key performance area may involve a lot of writing space. So your Job Performance Audit Form might be several pages long. Don't be alarmed about this. The main thing is to identify all the tasks relevant to the key performance area involved. If you end up with a book for one job or one employee, so be it.

The *Component Performance Objectives* column is for statements that are

JOB PERFORMANCE AUDIT FORM   Job: **Parcel courier**

Key Performance Area:	Care of vehicle	+	P	-	?
Outline of Tasks	**Component Performance Objectives**				
1. Start-up inspection	1.1 Walks slowly around the vehicle before entering to ensure that the tyres are properly inflated and bear no visible signs of damage, no suspicious leaks of fluid are visible, the body bears no signs of damage, the lenses of all lights are undamaged, and the wiper blades are correctly positioned and in good shape. This will normally take no more than one minute.	✓			
	1.2 Enters the vehicle to check the signal lamps, the headlamps, the tail lamps and brake lights, being sure to confirm that these lamps and lights flash or light on the outside. Normally this will be done in less than a minute.	✓			
	1.3 Inside the vehicle starts up the motor, checks the gauges and instruments to make sure fuel level is up, the oil pressure and brakes are all right, that the seat is adjusted properly, that the horn works, that the mileage on the odometer is the same as that recorded on the vehicle history at the end of the previous shift, and that the motor seems to be running properly. Usually this will occur within no more than three minutes.			✓	
	1.4 Confirms that all doors operate properly and that those that should be locked are locked. This will occur normally within one minute.			✓	
	1.5 In case of some problem being found during this start-up inspection, reports this problem immediately to the fleet foreman. This will occur within five minutes of the problem being found.			✓	

Figure 5.2 Job performance audit form

refinements of the task statements, or that, at times, encompass two or more task statements. Here's where you apply the essentials of wording a performance objective that are laid out in Chapter 3. In our example at Figure 5.2 we have five performance objectives listed for the key performance area of 'Start-up inspection'.

In working out the component performance objectives, you may need to elaborate very little on the task statements themselves. In these cases just make sure your performance statements clearly lay out the *what, how,* and *when* involved, as well as the required *standard(s).* (The required standards might also be referred to as the 'performance criteria'.)

The last four columns on the Job Performance Audit Form use a short form of symbols. Use these columns to check off the performance levels for the work group or individual concerned against the performance objective(s) for the job performance being audited. It's at this point that you really get down to the task of clearly identifying performance discrepancies, and is where the information you're using for placing your tick marks must be as accurate and objective as possible.

+	=	Performance level higher than required
P	=	Performance level as required
–	=	Performance level below what's required
?	=	Unknown performance level

In our example the last three performance objectives are marked as being below the required performance level or standard, meaning that they do not come up to the performance criteria involved. These clearly become the focus of concern about performance discrepancies, at least for this one task.

In looking at the job of parcel courier as a whole, we may have identified it as being made up of five key performance areas:

- delivery of parcels
- pick up of parcels
- care of vehicle
- provision of daily reports
- driving procedures

Our sample at Figure 5.2 focuses on one task within the key performance area of 'care of vehicle'. We will say that this KPA may involve the tasks of:

- start-up inspection
- prevention of vehicle damage
- maintenance of vehicle history form
- reporting of faults/damage
- end-of-shift inspection

From this list of tasks you can see that the sample at Figure 5.2 only dealt with the first task: 'start-up inspection'. Additional job audit pages would have to be made out for the other tasks so you could easily end up with five pages of tasks and performance objectives on the KPA of 'care of vehicle' alone.

Depending on the number of performance objectives involved for each task statement, you might have two or more tasks listed on the same page. It is always possible too that in the process of developing the performance objectives for the tasks, two or more tasks might fit into one performance objective. If this happens, then you must adjust your list of tasks accordingly, or list the tasks involved on the job performance audit form next to the one performance objective that covers all of them.

In deciding on your listing of component performance objectives, remember your task is to make things clearer through your analytical work, not murkier. Excessive detail or excessive attention to small and unimportant aspects of a job or task can bog you down. Clearly-stated and readily understandable performance objectives shed light for everyone.

Individual or Group?

The job performance audit process can focus on employees individually or on a given group of employees as a whole. The decision as to which route to pursue depends on the overall objective set for your training needs analysis work. In general, it probably makes sense most of the time to aim at the group. In some cases, however, perhaps because of the importance of the job involved or because of the importance of generating individual information, the individual approach could commend itself.

Setting Out the Performance Discrepancies

The last three performance objectives on our job performance audit form shown at Figure 5.2 were checked as not being up to the performance requirement. These objectives could be set out on their own separately as the performance discrepancies for the task of 'start-up inspection'. If you found that it was really a portion of the objective concerned that was not up to scratch, then you would take that portion and set it out as a performance discrepancy statement.

In our sample at Figure 5.2 the third objective reads:

Inside the vehicle starts up the motor, checks the gauges and instruments to make sure fuel level is up, the oil pressure and brakes are all right, that the seat is adjusted properly, that the horn works, that the mileage on the odometer is the same as that recorded on the vehicle history at the end of the previous shift, and that the motor seems to be running properly. Usually this will occur within no more than three minutes.

Suppose that the portion of this performance objective which is really the performance *problem* is that the employees do not check their gauges properly or listen to the motor running to ensure that it is not obviously misfiring. In this case the performance discrepancy statement might become:

Checks all gauges and instruments correctly and ensures that the motor is running properly. This will occur within no more than two minutes.

In examining this statement you need to decide whether it is all right on its own, or should remain part of the complete performance objective here, with the whole objective being declared a performance discrepancy.

Even though the other parts of the objective might be performed properly, it might make sense to include them, in case the employee should later get the impression that these other parts are no longer important for some reason or other.

In addition to thinking about a portion of the performance objective as opposed to the entire performance objective, you need to think about whether the performance set here should be included as a whole, even though the first two performance objectives checked out all right. Because there is a logical set here, it could make good sense to declare the whole set an area of performance discrepancy. This would prevent undue emphasis being placed in future action on three objectives at the potential expense of two.

Making this judgement call is part of your analytical work in clearly identifying the performance discrepancy here and in other parts of the complete process of setting out the performance discrepancies.

Apparent Reasons for Performance Discrepancies

This part of the training needs analysis process is pivotal. It's at this stage that you identify those discrepancies that might arise from inadequate training and those that might arise from other causes. Setting out the reasons here that link to *training* inadequacies, in effect, points directly at the training needs involved.

In noting the reasons for performance discrepancies, you run the risk of engaging in fault finding or finger pointing. If people are somehow at fault, directly or indirectly, knowingly or unknowingly, then the potential for political upheavals grows larger. Perhaps people think they're being pointed at, when, in fact, they are not. It's at this point that you may find your earlier 'contract' with the key decision maker for the training needs analysis process invaluable.

Small and subtle changes might be made in data. Other 'causes' might be advanced or hinted at. Threats of various kinds might emerge. At this point you have to be sure of your ground, and ready to support and defend your information. A certain degree of diplomacy combined with mental toughness becomes essential.

None of this should alarm you about the training needs analysis process. The chances are that no seriously negative reactions will arise. This will particularly be the case if you do a good job of planning and laying out the groundwork in the first place. When people clearly know what to expect ahead of time, and why it's really in their own best interests, they're not likely to go off the deep end in becoming hostile towards you or your colleagues.

Training or Education?

For our purposes, these two modes of instruction and organized learning differ. So if we've identified needs that can best be met by some form of education (eg academic upgrading, long-term professional improvement), those would be education needs and, in the structure of the training needs analysis process set out here, would likely have been identified as 'other needs' at the training needs identification stage. As noted before, this does not make them unimportant, it simply makes them different from training needs.

Some education needs, because they're so close to the borderline between education and training, might go through the filtering or refining process and end up being called training needs. In this case, they would be dealt with as part of the 'analysing the training needs' stage of the complete training needs analysis process.

In thinking about the difference between these two instructional or learning areas it might help to consider the diagram at Figure 5.3, which sets out the three critical areas of human learning. The biggest, and our base, of course, is simply our life experience, where we engage in an incredible amount of learning (and mislearning), often without realizing it. The middle layer is our education area, normally looked after by various types of formal educational institutions. Finally, we have training, which is closest to the actual work itself. A vital issue in these different layers is the degree of focus involved. And the focal point is actual work, or the job itself.

The diagram shows these three areas of human learning as being sharply divided. In actuality, of course, no such sharp divisions occur. It's more of a blending at the borders. Then too, in any one day you might learn something from life, learn something in an educational setting, and learn something from a training session. The arrows leading in and out of these levels help to indicate this interactive aspect. Note that the work itself is also part of our total learning process. This fits in with the

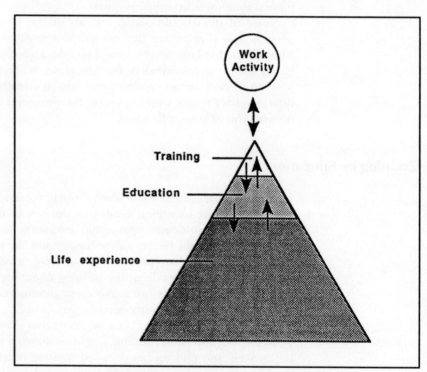

Figure 5.3 *The human learning pyramid*

kaizen concept mentioned in Chapter 1.

The following points of contrast may help to develop the distinction here a little more sharply:

Education	Training
• formal process	• generally informal
• institutional setting	• non-institutional setting
• outcomes usually specified in more generalized objectives	• outcomes can be specified as behavioural objectives
• generalized design	• applied design
• long-term process	• short-term process
• oriented to the person	• oriented to the job
• tends to be an organic form of learning	• tends to be a mechanistic form of learning
• theoretical and conceptual work often emphasized	• little emphasis on the theoretical or conceptual
• open to a wide range of people	• sharply-delineated target population, usually working in learning area concerned
• provides foundation for various unspecified behaviours	• specific behaviours set as outcomes
• professionally-accredited instructors	• mostly non-professional instructors
• may or may not involve some direct application 'some day'	• intended for direct application immediately or relatively soon

Having set these points out, once again it is important to stress that they're not hard and fast. The same instructors might provide either education or training. Some training could take place in an institutional setting. Similarly, some education programmes could occur in or near a work setting. Some training programmes might contain education elements, and some education programmes might contain training elements. The key issue here is to work on developing a 'feel' for which is which.

In the training needs analysis perspective, we need to be as clear as possible about what is training and what is education, the former being our main concern here. But we have to accept that often it's going to be a toss-up as to which is which in a given situation. And this area of toss-up will often have an important bearing on the results of the training needs analysis process.

The Training Needs

These are areas of performance discrepancy that, in your judgement, can best be remedied with some kind of training. As part of your analytical work at this stage you must find out or point out why other kinds of interventions would not be as effective as training in removing these discrepancies.

Consider such possible courses of action as better job guides, better information flow, improved management or supervision, changes in equipment or work location, existing education programmes and so on. (Remember the listing shown on the diagram at Figure 1.3 on p. 23.) Be fair in your work at this point. You might even find it helpful to use the basic options comparison matrix (Figure 4.2, p. 54). On this matrix you could plot different performance discrepancy areas across the top as 'factors', with different methods being listed down the page on the left. Then you could clearly sort out the virtues of the different methods against the identified discrepancies.

Because the number of methods could be large, you would need to modify the matrix layout to accommodate them. In some cases you might winnow out potential methods in a general way before using the matrix format, in order to end up with a more manageable listing of methods.

One winnowing process could simply involve examining a list of possible causes of performance discrepancies and the potential actions (based on Figure 1.3), and eliminating or including them according to your general knowledge of all the performance discrepancies identified. If this were done in unison with a team of people who had been involved in the analysis work, so much the better.

When you identify performance needs other than training needs, try to set out some general directions for meeting them. A reference to methods that should be examined other than training would be most helpful to your decision maker and other key people in the work group or organization.

After all of this sorting and winnowing work, what you have left are your training needs. Referring to our earlier panning for gold analogy in Chapter 1, this is your gold. Now you need to decide how to refine it.

TRAINER'S TIPS

1. Take special care to make good use of your first contacts with new clients.
2. Always work carefully to build solid working relationships with the key people involved in the training needs analysis process.
3. Whenever important decisions are involved, always look for tangible commitments.
4. In carrying out the training needs analysis process, delegate as much of the work as you reasonably can to other people.
5. Ensure that task outlines exist for all tasks identified as particularly important to the training needs analysis process.
6. Ensure that people understand that performance discrepancies should not be dealt with as 'failings' on the part of certain individuals.
7. When specific areas of doubt exist concerning actual performance quality, strive to use 'on-the-job observation' as part of your information-gathering.
8. Make sure that the people you're working with do not use the terms 'education' and 'training' interchangeably.
9. At all times work to help people understand that not all training needs will necessarily justify setting up training courses.
10. Never underestimate the value of producing well-written reports or delivering solid presentations to deal with key junctures of the training needs analysis process.

Analysing the Training Needs

Once you have your training needs, you can examine them closely from a training perspective. It's all very well to say that training is required, but what kind of training, delivered by whom, how, where and why? More analysis!

In starting your analysis of the training needs, set out a number of questions for yourself. Here are some questions that might well apply to each training need in turn:

1. Does this need apply right across the work group, department or organization?
2. Does this need apply to just one particular group of employees in a given location?
3. Does this need apply only to one or several individuals?
4. Is this need an anticipated one (proactive)?

5. Is this need one that arises out of present performance short-comings (reactive)?
6. Does this training need involve some form of specialized knowledge or skill that might make it difficult to learn for someone in the target population?
7. Is this need centred directly on an identifiable job, or is it more global?
8. Will accomplishment of this training objective by the individual or group of people concerned be cost effective for the organization as a whole?

You can think of more questions in a similar vein. Given the particular training needs analysis process you're involved with, certain questions are likely to emerge quite clearly as a direct result of the process itself. Here again some form of matrix layout for the training needs against your questions could prove helpful.

The diagram shown at Figure 5.4 lays out the field to keep in mind as you examine each training need. Keeping this field in mind will help you sharpen your focus on each training need, thereby making your recommendation for dealing with it sharper and more useful to the organization.

The *make-up of the workforce* involved is important, because it clearly sets out the human resources you have to work with in achieving the training need. Such factors as age, education, experience, general morale and so on could all have a bearing on the likely success of prospective training. Here you might also take into account promises made to individual employees or groups of employees, especially in the case of those who might only recently have been recruited into the company.

External influences could cover quite a range. They really only need to be dealt with if they clearly impinge on, or are likely to impinge on, the training need you're examining. Such factors as government funding for training, ready availability of certain relevant training courses in an institution or another organization, or even legally-mandated training requirements, might all have influence here.

The *organizational structure* might well have an important bearing on a training need. Will a production line have to be closed down if people in a given area receive training? Will the training of one group or individual affect others? Is the organization centralized, or is it widely scattered in relatively small units? This could influence whether training might be delivered centrally, or have to be delivered with some form of a 'travelling road show'.

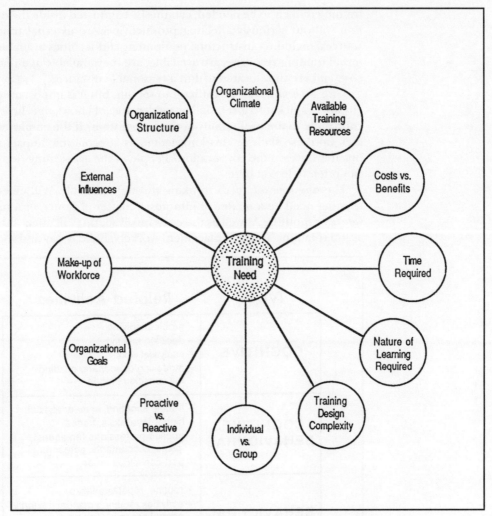

Figure 5.4 *The training need decision field*

Consider the *organizational climate.* Is training of any kind normally regarded positively? Or is it dealt with reluctantly? Has the company been enjoying recent market success? Or is it a time of retrenchment? (In times of retrenchment you can sometimes make an even more compelling case for training.)

What of your *available training resources?* Is there a training department? Does it have the competence and size needed for the training need concerned? Are training locations suitably equipped? If on-the-job training is likely to be needed, can this be conducted inside the organization without seriously affecting productivity? Are external training resources, including instructors, equipment and facilities available? If external training resources are available, are they available at a reasonable cost, and are they located within a reasonable distance?

Costs vs. benefits can be difficult to set out, but it is important to try. If employees pick up a given skill or a given area of knowledge, how will this contribute to the profitability of the corporation? If the employees don't pick up these skills or this knowledge, what economic impact will this possibly have on the corporation? People in the accounting department can often help you here.

The *time required* needs thinking through carefully. Will meeting the training need be a matter of minutes, a matter of hours, or a matter of weeks or months? As well as the costs involved, this will affect such issues as job rotations, use of replacement workers, holiday pay and so forth.

Type	Related Activities
COGNITIVE	– problem solving – decision making – analytical work – modelling or scenario building – full conscious mode
COGNITIVE/ BEHAVIOURAL	– trouble shooting, semi-analytical – higher-level skills, trades – applied professions (engineers, pilots, accountants, surgeons) – part-conscious mode
BEHAVIOURAL	– routine, repetitive tasks – activities requiring manual dexterity – normal assembly line work – work open to robotic design – non-conscious mode

Figure 5.5 *Key learning domains*

The *nature of learning required* is an important issue. It will have a direct impact on the training methods used. Lectures, videocassettes, discussions, tests, readings, programmed instruction, computer-assisted instruction, on-the-job instruction and the like might come into consideration here. The diagram at Figure 5.5 shows one way in which a training need might be analysed from this perspective.

In using the Key Learning Domains chart, you need to determine which of the domains applies to the training need under examination. Most learning methods lend themselves to the cognitive/behavioural domain. Only true 'hands on' methods lend themselves to the full behavioural domain. Some methods such as lecture and demonstration seem to be the preserve of the fully cognitive domain. In making these sweeping kinds of statements, of course, don't let yourself ignore learning possibilities that involve actually doing what is required by the training need. With the cognitive domain, for instance, some means of determining whether or not people can actually think or analyse is needed somewhere along the line.

The next diagram, Figure 5.6, gives you a further means of analysing a given training need. The learning impact hierarchy enables you to think about the potential training location from the perspective of its nearness to the job as well as the learning domain involved.

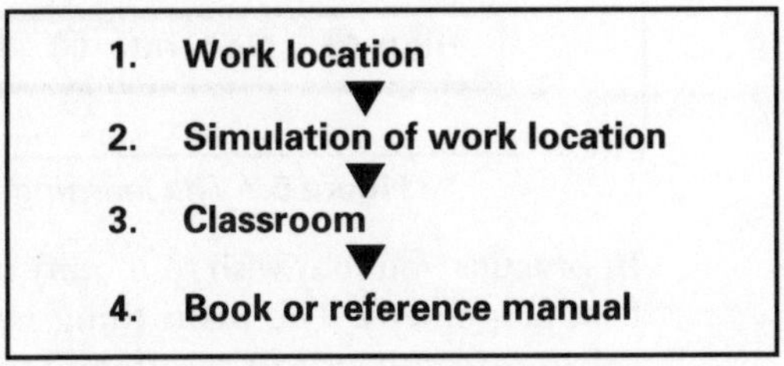

```
┌─────────────────────────────────────────────┐
│   1.   Work location                          │
│                  ▼                            │
│   2.   Simulation of work location            │
│                  ▼                            │
│   3.   Classroom                              │
│                  ▼                            │
│   4.   Book or reference manual               │
└─────────────────────────────────────────────┘
```

Figure 5.6 *The learning impact hierarchy*

In a general sense, the actual work location is your best learning location for training. This applies particularly to skills and knowledge of the behavioural type. Some behavioural learning lends itself well to simulation types of learning (including computer simulations), but the classroom is a doubtful arena for this type of learning (unless learning materials are very practical, and are available for each learner). Some   of the cognitive/ behavioural learning requirements can be met effectively in the actual work location, but they will probably need the 'reflective' space offered by simulation types of learning as well as classroom learning.

Some of this you can work through using the Learning Domain/ Impact Matrix shown at Figure 5.7. This matrix is not completely objective in its allocation of relative weights to the impact levels for the learning domains involved, but it does force thinking along these lines.

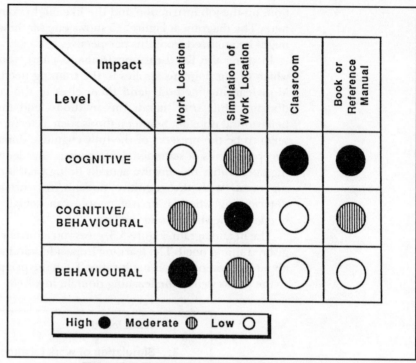

Figure 5.7 *The learning domain/impact matrix*

In practice you may wish to modify these weights according to your own best judgement. The main thing is to ensure that your judgement involves care and at least an attempt to remain objective.

One thing this matrix will do is to force you away from allotting any one learning impact area automatically to a given training need simply because it is readily available. Availability of this kind may have a certain convenience appeal, but it could well involve the wrong kind of learning for the need involved.

In considering training needs from the perspective of the 'nature of learning' it is also important to consider the possible involvement of performance sets as training needs. Conceivably, a training need set could require training methods and locations that will require all three key learning domains and all four learning impact areas. This need not complicate things unduly. All it means is that the given aspects of the training need set (eg individual training objectives that are components of the set) might need different learning treatments. So a given training module might require different levels and domains at different stages of its conduct.

If you eventually conduct a training programme in, say, using explosives, it might well involve reading assignments, classroom work, simulation training, and eventually actual placement and detonation of explosives. Cognitive, cognitive/behavioural and behavioural learning domains would all come into play at different stages. These different stages would most likely be conducted in different locations suited to the programme aspect involved. In this kind of training, for instance, you probably wouldn't want to risk blowing up the classroom!

In working with the Training Need Decision Field, or analysing the training needs you've uncovered, the process of sorting out the nature of the learning required must not receive short shrift. This point requires stressing, because so many training programmes, training organizations and training institutes exist that you might otherwise be tempted to 'force fit' a training need into an inappropriate training activity for convenience, or because of pressure being exerted by various authorities. This is an area where you must stand your ground based on the value of your analytical work.

In considering the nature of the learning required, take care also to distinguish as carefully as you can between educational resources and activities, and training resources and activities. Remember the distinctions between education and training laid out earlier.

Going back to the chart, The Training Need Decision Field (Figure 5.4), the issue of *training design complexity* now comes into consideration. Some training needs might require quite simple training programmes. Others could require longer-range programmes involving a number of different subject areas. Less complex design needs could well lie within the capabilities of the organization concerned. More involved designs could probably require outside assistance.

Once again you could easily find yourself involved with questions of training versus education. A complex design might require an intermingling of both, including a mix of on-the-job and classroom work. Some apprenticeship programmes are very much of this type, taking advantage of both educational institutions and training departments.

Very complicated training designs might even point to the need to set up broad new areas of education and training which could eventually give rise to new fields of technology or professional practice.

The issue of *individual versus group* brings up the point of whether or not the training need in question focuses on one or two specific people, or an entire class of worker. Here again, you need to take care in selecting the right approach. While some people might think it a good idea to 'take advantage' of a training programme to include people for whom it was not directly intended, this can be an expensive advantage. It could easily end up training people in tasks or jobs they will never use, with consequent frustrations and loss of productivity.

In considering the area of *proactive versus reactive*, the key question is whether or not the training need arises from anticipated work requirements (eg those involved in setting up a new factory or a new production line), or from actual performance problems or discrepancies occurring right now in the workplace.

How soon will on-the-job application be needed? If a new work procedure won't come into effect for at least a year, it won't make much sense to engage in a one-week training programme right now in anticipation. By the time the new procedure begins, people will have forgotten most of what they had learned. As a rule of thumb it makes sense to try to have people able to apply their new skills and knowledge well within a month of the termination of the relevant training. Ideally, they should be able to apply their new learning almost immediately.

In reactive situations, people will most likely have the opportunity to use what they've learned very quickly.

In proactive situations, things become a bit less definite. Delays in opening a new factory or office can affect things, as too can unexpected dips in the economy or unforeseen events of various types. Given these uncertainties, the best one can do is to make reasonably-informed guesses or estimates and do one's best to ensure the quick on-the-job application of planned training.

Organizational goals can have a major impact on whether or not, or how, you might meet training needs. If a reactive training need exists to help employees overcome a performance problem, but that problem exists in an area of corporate operation that will soon be phased out, there's probably not much value in providing training. The problem will disappear anyway, so you need not get into the trap of training for yesterday's needs.

Given the importance of organizational goals, clear lines of communication with senior management must exist. Otherwise, detailed planning could take place to meet needs that are beside the point, with all the consequent waste of money and time.

Analysing the training needs involved in the training needs analysis process can involve a lot of work. But it is essential work for building the right training design to meet the needs uncovered. And if you don't end up with the right training designs, the whole process of training needs analysis can turn out to be pointless.

Training Objectives

Given the earlier work on performance objectives, the training objectives should fall into place naturally and easily. The details of this process were brought out in Chapter 3. As noted in that chapter, some work might still be required to smooth out the performance objectives to ensure that they translate well into training objectives.

In setting out the training objectives, you must rely heavily on your analysis of the training needs. This will help you to sort out hierarchies that might be at work (eg meeting one objective before going on to tackle another, or setting out overall objectives with sub-objectives). Similarly, in larger undertakings, you may have to deal with course or programme objectives for logical groupings of training objectives. This would relate to the eventual organization of training modules or larger training programmes with various levels of accomplishment.

If, for some reason, earlier work in setting out performance objectives has not been complete, the training objectives stage becomes all the more important. You must ensure that objectives clearly specify the learning required, the standards, and the learning times. All must meet the requirements of the job as brought out in the training needs identification work.

Further work in task analysis might come into play here. Earlier work at the task outline or job performance audit levels might not have specified given actions precisely enough. In some cases, detailed work of this kind might not have occurred earlier for a variety of reasons. Whatever has gone on earlier, the training objectives stage represents the last chance clearly to specify what must actually and precisely be included in the required training. You cannot skip over this stage or deal with it in a perfunctory way.

Recommended Training Design

This design (which can include components of education or be conducted entirely within an educational institution), must lay out all the required learning for all the individuals or work groups dealt with in the training needs analysis process. The time specifications become critical here. Will a one-hour session suffice to meet a given training need? Or will several weeks be required to meet the requirements of a given cluster of training objectives? Less frequently, you may have to specify year-by-year progressions in the case of various kinds of learnership, apprenticeship or professional training programmes.

When educational institutions of various kinds are involved, you must show what, exactly, they will provide. Will employees need to travel to evening classes at a local polytechnic? Will they take distance learning programmes from a university? Will teachers or professors come to the work location? Travel arrangements, accommodation, classroom allocations, meals, audiovisual requirements, equipment requirements and so on, must all come into consideration.

In effect, the end of the training needs analysis process becomes the beginning of the complete training design process. The former points out the objectives and goals required, and the types of training or education needed. The latter goes more completely into making the final arrangements including precise indications of learners, instructors, dates, locations, and costs.

The Training Needs Analysis Report

From time to time I have mentioned the need for a report in dealing with the whole training needs analysis process. In considering what we've gone over so far in this book you can see that there are a number of points where reports might make sense. Indeed, management, or some other authority may demand such reports.

Executive summary
Introduction
Background
Scope
Method(s)
Findings
Analysis
Conclusions
Recommendations
Appendixes

Figure 5.8 *Training needs analysis report format*

The easiest way to show a useful structure for this report is to set out a format model for the key sections you could logically include. You have this at Figure 5.8.

The *executive summary* lays out the detail of the entire report in capsule form. It should not take more than one page, and preferably no more than half a page. It should give the reader the bare bones of what has been done and the resulting recommendations. After reading it, the reader should understand the essence of what the entire report covers.

The *introduction* lets the reader know the general layout of the report and the reasons for organizing it this way. It should give fuller details than the executive summary and get the reader properly started into the main structure of the report.

In the *background* section you let the reader know the history that led up to the training needs analysis process being dealt with. This can include details of dates, people, decisions and the like. In some cases you may logically blend the introduction and background together.

Your reader receives depth and breadth indicators in the *scope*. What target population or populations did you deal with? What location or locations came under study? How extensive and detailed was your analytical work? In this section, too, you would set out your terms of reference, clearly showing the what, who, why and when of your work, as well as the authority given to you to conduct the work required.

The *method(s)* section must leave the reader with a thorough understanding of how the training needs analysis process was carried out, including the reasons for the method or methods used. This section too could be a logical one for detailing all the people involved in conducting the complete analysis.

The *findings* are critical. You may wish to subdivide this section into findings that concern performance discrepancies, those involving identified training needs, and those dealing with the analysis of the training needs. Considerations such as numbers involved, relative importance of findings, unique anomalies and so on will help you decide whether or not subdividing makes sense here.

The *analysis* section of the report should highlight the various analyses carried out during the training needs analysis process. It must certainly deal with such considerations as implications of various aspects of the study, arguments pro and con certain viewpoints that might be adopted in light of the information uncovered, evidence of careful judgements at work, and various other points that will help the reader to understand the reasoning processes engaged in during the conduct of the entire training needs analysis process.

The *conclusions* section sets out those conclusions you can fairly and logically draw from the findings and the analysis of those findings. Normally, you should set the conclusions out in a point-form list. This makes it easier to review them and refer to them from time to time. In setting out your list of conclusions, you should ensure that they are organized by priority and areas of performance or training concerned. Most of the time a priority order of highest-to-lowest works best in the point-form list.

The *recommendations* section should flow logically from the conclusions, but not necessarily on a one-to-one basis. Again, a point-form list of recommendations makes sense. These should be worded crisply and point to definite actions, complete with time/date references where possible.

In the *appendixes* part of the report you can list all those detailed forms or data sheets that support the work reported, but which do not necessarily merit inclusion in the body of the report. Such appendixes will probably receive mention at appropriate points in the body of the report. An appendix is a logical place to include such references as job or position descriptions, task outlines, factors charts and options comparison charts. Here you might also include technical drawings, photographs, organization charts, government or training board guidelines, employee survey documents of various kinds, site blueprints and so forth.

Your report does not necessarily have to follow the format outline suggested here in exact detail. You should think it through and deliberately decide what to include and what not to include before sitting down actually to write the report. In addition, remember to think about a suitable report cover, the setting out of a good title page, and a table of contents. In some cases, it might be useful for you to include an index. Think, too, about the possibility of including a glossary of terms to help the reader understand all the technical terms used.

Related Presentations

Usually you will have to make various presentations in connection with various aspects of the training needs analysis process. We've already noted that you might have to do this to gain acceptance for various approaches you plan to take at or near the beginning of the whole process. At various other times you may also be asked to make presentations.

The main thing to keep in mind here is that you don't always have to make the same kind of presentation. Sometimes you can be informal, and other times formal. Judge your audiences and the settings, and decide what you want each of your presentations to achieve for you and for the training needs analysis process.

Consider using such resources as overhead transparencies, charts, posters, models, information sheets and the like to supplement or support your presentations. Often, you'll be able to dip directly into samples of your analytical work to date to flesh out your presentations effectively.

When you reach the end of the training needs analysis process, as part of working on your final report, keep in mind the need for making more than one presentation with the same information. At times you may need to deliver preliminary reports as presentations. Similarly, when the report itself is complete, you may want to use it directly as a reference for one or more of your presentations about the training needs analysis work that has been done.

Often, when you're making these working kinds of presentations you may need to remind yourself of the need to make links from one to the next. This may occur in a serial fashion as the training needs analysis work unfolds. Sometimes, too, you may need to make the same or similar presentations to ever higher levels of people in the work group or organization you're dealing with. Here it's important to keep firmly in mind the various decision-making implications that might be involved.

Careful Analysis

This chapter has gone over a number of points in detail that will help you to conduct the full-scale training needs analysis process. In looking at all the details given here you may, at times, feel more than a little overwhelmed. The natural question that will arise is: 'Will it all be worth it?' The answer, in the main, is 'yes'.

Not every client or every department or every organization will work effectively with the analytical work you do. Some people may even brush aside all your hard efforts. But the fact remains that if you conduct the work professionally and thoroughly in the first place, it will stand as an undeniable testimonial to your integrity and authority. If your work isn't accepted quickly, it will, at least, have staying power, and the right kind of staying power will count solidly for your reputation.

Conduct your analytical work responsibly and correctly and you will serve the interests of both your clients and yourself. You will certainly stake out a position for yourself as part of the solution, not part of the problem.

▶   QUESTIONS FOR THE ANALYST   ◀

- On first going in to a given work group or organization, what key things would you personally want to clarify and obtain agreement on with your client from the start?
- In the past when you've worked with someone acting as your liaison person for a given task or project, what specific pros and cons of the relationship came into play?
- Think of a task or project you'll be involved with in the future. Where will your 'operating base' for this task be? What specific things can you do to make this base as useful to you as possible?
- What examples of functional or operational fixedness have you encountered in the past?
- In carrying out a training needs analysis task within your own organization, where would you see the need to provide spoken or written reports to the decision makers involved?
- Think of a specific work area you've had involvement with in the past. Can you set out at least one performance discrepancy you can recall from that experience in your own performance or in the performance of someone else?
- Which jobs or work areas that you have experience with would lend themselves to being broken down readily, using the format of the Job Performance Audit Form?
- What are some of the specific reasons you can think of that explain why the words *education* and *training* are so often used interchangeably?
- Which key learning domain has most often been involved in providing the training you've been involved with in the past?
- What exemplifies at least one good training objective for an area of work with which you are familiar?

6
Getting the Information

▷   SUMMARY   ◁

This chapter:

- Provides pointers for identifying your information sources in a work group or organization and sets out the need for establishing an information-accessing plan.
- Sets out practical hints for improved attentiveness in different settings. It notes important points about conducting interviews and describes practical ways to relate better to your client while gathering information.
- Goes into many details concerning the design, distribution and use of questionnaires to gather information. Six practical and easy-to-follow examples of different types of questionnaires are provided. Tips for sampling are given, including the best respondent mix to use.
- Provides a detailed examination of the use and value of the nominal group method.
- Describes the Delphi technique and its value in gathering good information. The use of key term analysis in research is included and how to deal with the outcomes is shown.
- Details the ways in which the dynamic classification chart can be used to sort information of all kinds, including practical diagrams to illustrate.
- Sets out important tips for keeping yourself on track during the important search for information.

Going After the Information

We have now gone over the key issues and methods involved in the full training needs analysis process. Within that process a major consideration is obtaining good information from people at various levels in the organization, an important part of your research.

Each method or technique you use has its own merits and its own best applications. The important thing is to understand how they work and be able to use them to best advantage in the full flow of your work.

Discussions, meetings, interviews, on-the-job observations, reviews of job descriptions, various kinds of employee surveys and applied thinking are all important, and require time and support from the key decision makers involved. Depending on the importance of the people whose work is analysed, a thorough job of analysis might take the better part of a year. In the case of fully-fledged trades or professions, the necessary analytical work could easily take several years. Everyone taking part must understand this and be prepared to give the necessary commitments.

Identifying Your Information Resources

Once you are clear about the different aspects you will need to deal with in the planned training needs analysis process, you must identify and connect with all the human and material resources that can provide you with information. Talking with various key people will help you do this as will a review of various books, manuals or other documents.

Ask yourself these questions:

1. Which people inside the organization are likely to have useful information about the work area or areas I or we will be looking into?
2. What information sources such as libraries, files, databases and the like exist that could prove helpful?
3. What sources outside the target organization might provide good information? (Consider machinery manufacturers, trade and professional organizations, government bodies, polytechnics or universities.)

In thinking through your likely sources, be sure to review organization charts and various corporate publications and follow up on the leads you find along the way.

As you find your sources, arrange to have contact with them or to be able to review the materials involved. In doing this draw up a contact list complete with names, phone numbers and locations. Make notes about the areas of expertise linked to each person. Make a similar list for your material sources, being sure to note the likely quality of each source you list.

Doing a good job of setting out your information resources at the start will repay dividends in the long haul. If you're working as a group, be sure that each member of the analysing group has a copy of all the identified resources.

Arranging Times and Places

When you've got a good idea of the information resources available and notes about how to access them, start making arrangements to meet them or to review materials. Consider such priority issues as organizational pecking orders, source quality, availability, convenience of location and the like in drawing up your meeting and reading schedule.

If you're working as a group, arrange for specific members of your team to meet with specific resource people or to review specific resource documents. As part of this, you will also want to arrange meetings of your team from time to time to go over your findings and to revise or update your information-gathering work.

Whether you're working alone or as a group, relate your information planning work to your training needs analysis process plan as described in Chapter 4. And, once again, keep in mind that the action appraisal technique could help you to think through and set up your information-accessing plan.

Attentiveness

In all aspects of the training needs analysis process you must remain alert to all the information possibilities wherever you go. This includes making sure your listening skills remain sharp, being observant, actually performing some key tasks, listening and looking for the things that haven't been spelled out for you or shown to you, checking things out for yourself when you have doubts, and always being ready to ask questions. At times you may even find it pays to play the role of 'complete dummy'. Most people can't resist showing off their skills or knowledge to a duffer (provided they have the time).

Pay attention as you meet people, view equipment or work processes, and visit different locations. By remaining deliberately attentive you can pick up all sorts of valuable information. You detect the undertones. You ferret out hidden agendas. You learn to appreciate the importance of what's not said. You spot unusual occurrences or detect strange anomalies. In essence, you work to turn your brain into an information sponge.

Equip yourself with the right tools to do your information-accessing job. A notebook is a must. Think of the importance of a notebook to a police constable; it's no less important to you, so keep your notebook with you at all times.

A camera or an audiotape recorder might be helpful. The same thing applies to using a videotape camera (camcorder). In using electronic recording equipment, of course, you have to remain sensitive to the likely reactions of the people you'll be dealing with. Generally it would not be advisable to make such recordings surreptitiously. Additionally, be sure to carry a briefcase, and consider whether or not you should have a safety hat readily available.

Cultivate the habit of attentiveness. Here are a number of points to bear in mind to help you do this:

1. Keep in mind a general orienting structure for all that you're interested in probing into.
2. Be careful about letting others show you too willingly what they want to show you.
3. Pick up on key words used by the people you're talking to and use these to frame deeper questions or as the basis for obtaining additional information.
4. Open yourself up to hearing, seeing and feeling things at all your levels of reception — emotional, figurative, hands on, visual, and so on.
5. When possible, pick up information resources you come across by chance (eg other people to meet, sketches, diagrams, slides, photographs, audiotapes, videotapes, technical data sheets, technical manuals, production sheets, spare equipment or tools etc.).
6. Avoid making quick judgements about what you see, hear or touch. Allow yourself reflection time.
7. Don't let your personal feelings get in the way of accurately picking up on the information available.
8. Make it easy for people to talk to you or to show you things.
9. Don't allow extraneous noises or activities to capture your attention. Deliberately fix your mind on the information area you need to review.
10. If you're unsure about the correctness of a given item of information, make a note to yourself, and be sure to check it out with other sources.
11. Summarize the information you receive from each of your information sources. (Remember your notebook.)
12. Remain flexible about your information sources at all times.

In obtaining information, you're an investigator. So keep in mind all the attributes of a good investigator in any field. In this way, you're most likely to obtain the right information in the right ways at the right times.

Whatever you do, remain open to the information possibilities. Hunches will often serve you well. Remain flexible at all times.

Conducting Interviews

One of the most frequent modes of communication you're likely to use in gathering the information you need is the interview. You may interview people at the same level as yourself in the organization, people at a lower level, or people at high levels, up to and including the top. So you have to prepare yourself to ensure you conduct all the interviews you require in a fully professional manner.

Interviews might take place casually as one-to-one encounters. They may take place in more formal or structured ways. They might involve yourself as one interviewer, or yourself as one of a team of interviewers. In the people you interview you may find friendliness and openness, evasiveness, or downright hostility, and this can occur all in the same interview session!

For the more casual types of interviews it's wise to prepare yourself in general terms. You never know when a chance conversation in the canteen or on the bus, or an encounter in the parking area will become a casual interview. Have some key questions ready that you always want to ask at the drop of a hat. For dealing with the casual situations too, be sure that you've armed yourself well with the cautions or touchy areas to avoid or treat with extra care. You want to do your best not to stir up antagonisms.

In getting ready for any type of interview you'll find the points in the following list helpful either generally in the case of casual interviews, or as specific points to deal with in more formal interviews:

1. Ensure in your own mind that the interview is likely to give you worthwhile information regarding performance requirements and short falls, or the specific analytical information you're seeking.
2. Think through clearly what information you want to obtain from the interview, keeping things as specific as possible. As part of this decide if using specific job or position descriptions, technical information, the Job Performance Audit Form or other documents would make sense in the interview.
3. Decide whether your interview will work best with a single individual or a panel doing the interview, and proceed with the rest of your planning accordingly.
4. If possible, arrange for the interview to take place in a quiet, private, and comfortable location.
5. Give the person or people you'll be interviewing a clear idea ahead of time of what you want to accomplish from the interview — something in writing could be worthwhile to help in this explanation.

6. Ensure that you prepare a list of key points of information you wish to obtain during the interview (this list could overlap with any written work you send beforehand to the person or people you're interviewing). As part of this, it could a good idea to write out specific questions you plan to ask during the interview.
7. Plan to have plenty of time for the interview.
8. Ensure that you have your notebook with you for entering key items of information as they come up during the interview — a checklist of some kind makes good sense here.
9. Prepare all the resources you'll need during the interview, including manuals, slides, flipcharts, drawings, etc.
10. Plan your follow-up to the interview ahead of time, at least in general terms. This could include preparing an outline of the information you'll give to the person or group you've interviewed to give them a record of what you took from the interview and some idea of what you'll be doing next in your analytical work.

Interviews designed to bring out performance information take on many of the characteristics of business meetings. They need agendas and they need good control. At the same time, they can't become 'interrogation' sessions. You must handle things with a good level of tact, sometimes allowing others to carry the responsibility for acting as the leaders of these sessions. But you must never lose sight of the importance of being clear and specific about the questions you need answered, even if someone else does the asking. And don't be shy about taking the time to note information down accurately, sometimes asking people to repeat things to ensure that you have understood properly.

In conducting the interviews try always to do the following:

1. Start things off in a calm, business-like manner. Introduce yourself and any other members of the interviewing team.
2. Lay out how you plan to proceed carefully and specifically.
3. Solicit support from the person or people you're interviewing for the approach you plan to take and for the information outcomes you're looking for, but don't be too long or too anxious in doing this. You may just have to proceed even if the feelings aren't all supportive.
4. Go over the concept of performance objectives, performance discrepancies, training objectives, or other terms that may be relevant to the interview (an information sheet of some kind could be useful for this).
5. Make the first question you pose as straightforward as possible.

6. Phrase all your questions as plainly, specifically, and briefly as possible.
7. Allow a reasonable amount of time for the response or responses to your questioning, being sure to listen carefully. Be ready here to ask immediate further questions to expand on the answer you've been given — but beware of appearing to hector.
8. Avoid using rhetorical questions, putting words into people's mouths or phrasing your questions so they appear to call for certain answers (leading questions).
9. Keep in mind the need to reassure the other person or people from time to time that you relate, at least to some degree, to the concerns and feelings they express. (And be sincere about this.)
10. Now and then make positive (but sincere) comments about the information contributions being given to you.
11. When useful points emerge, build on them as necessary, through putting them in your own words for clarification ('As I understand what you're saying ...'), or through asking additional questions.
12. By all means resort to using a whiteboard or flipchart to write down specific points that need full and open discussion.
13. Be careful about expressing judgements or making evaluative comments during the interview.
14. End the interview on a positive and friendly note, being sure to let the other person or people know where things go from here. (This could include arranging for a further interview session.)
15. Immediately after the interview write down its highlights, being sure to note down key points you need to find out or the actions you need to take as a result of this session.
16. In the case of groups or teams of interviewers, be sure that everyone talks about the interview session and reaches some sort of general agreement about its worth. In some cases, it will make good sense to have one person produce an interview summary for all interviewers.

In posing questions during an interview, keep in mind that you should not pose certain types of questions. Probing into matters of age, race, even specific employment background could become quite tricky. In some cases you might even be contravening the law. If you're in doubt about a given question, clear it with someone in personnel or human resources who is in the know about human rights. If you can't check the question out with someone, and you have some doubts about its propriety, then don't ask it.

Well-conducted interviews are invaluable to the training needs analysis process. They can come into play at any stage. They require care and sensitivity in their conduct. Be wary about just letting them happen. Their potential value is too important for that.

Your Client's Perspective

Much depends on your client's perspective. Who is your client? Will you be dealing with one client or several? Will she, he or they be willing to share information with you accurately and comfortably? Or will you be forced to engage in verbal sparring a lot of the time? The answers to these questions will go far towards revealing how likely you are to succeed in pinpointing the critical performance issues and needs involved.

In some cases your client will be the person in charge of the organization or organizational unit you're dealing with. In other cases your clients will be the different managers you must deal with in various departments of the same organization. Sometimes you'll have clients at different levels of the hierarchy. No matter who they are, or where they fit in the overall scheme of things, you must work with them effectively to obtain useful and credible results.

It is often a good idea to treat anyone you interview as a client. This can help to ensure that you convey the right sense of respect and appreciation.

In working to make sure your client is as cooperative as possible with you and your information-gathering or evaluation process, observe the following steps:

1. Set out your thoughts and information clearly for the client.
2. Present a well-groomed appearance at all times.
3. Look for ways to set out your information attractively (graphs, colours, charts, etc.).
4. Give your client a good sense of personal involvement in what's going on.
5. Work to make your client feel that time spent with you is worthwhile.
6. Set out your communications so that clients will be able to pull out the salient points for themselves easily and accurately.
7. Ensure that the proceedings you describe and initiate build in a clear sense of direction.
8. Look for ways to give your client a clear sense of accomplishment.
9. Be brief and accurate in what you say without being blunt or curt.

10. When speaking, use a voice that has some sense of life and vigour.
11. Continually work at making sure your work and the approach you're using create a good impression.
12. Always be sure to work with your client on an adult-to-adult basis. Never appear to be 'talking down'.
13. Ensure that you thank your client properly for all the information he or she provides.

Using Tests

Assessing a trainee's performance in terms of knowledge, skill and attitude against set criteria for the job is an accepted method of identifying training needs. There are many jobs which involve people who have to maintain a particular qualifying standard. For example, first aiders may be required to take tests either annually or bi-annually in order to maintain the necessary standard. Performance appraisal on the job can clarify whether the actual or potential job performance discrepancy, which gave rise to the initial training need has been closed.

To many trainers the terms *assessment* or *test* mean only an end-of-course test, but in order constantly to maintain useful information regarding the analysis of training needs, it should be a continuous process. A number of testing techniques can be used:

Measuring the acquisition of knowledge

Short Answers
Answer the following questions:

- List Handy's cultures of an organization
- Define the term 'management'

The answers to questions such as these are unlikely to vary to any great extent, therefore making the marking relatively easy.

Multiple-Choice Questions
In coming up with choices in the multiple-choice questionnaire, work to make them seem like credible choices, at least at first glance. You don't want the correct response to stand out because it's the only likely one. Look out too for other ways in which the correct answer might stand out. Don't make it noticeably shorter or longer than the other choices. The same thing applies to word choice.

107

Each of the following statements is followed by a choice of four different possible answers. Signify which of the four choices for each statement, in your opinion, gives the correct definition by entering a tick mark.

1. The word 'hygroscopic' means:

    (a) Suitable for use in a dry environment. ❏
    (b) The attribute of humid adhesion in materials. ❏
    (c) Tending to absorb moisture from the air. ❏
    (d) Unstable on any metallic surface when wet. ❏
          etc.

Figure 6.1 *Multiple-choice question sample*

In general, make sure you vary which choice is the correct one in succeeding questions.

Completion/Deletion Questions

These consist of a single question which contains one or more blanks which the trainee has to complete either by inserting the correct word or words, or by deleting alternative words which do not relate to the correct answer. For example:

- Complete the following statement:
  A thermometer measures_____.
- Delete the words in brackets which do not apply :
  A tachometer measures (road speed/engine speed).

Matching Pairs

The trainee is presented with two lists of words or words and illustrations. Each item in one list can be paired with an item from the second list which the trainee has to identify. One list has more items than the other, so the chance of finding the correct answer by process of elimination is reduced.

Measuring the acquisition of skills

If the trainees display particular skills in their job, the measurement must reflect the relevant skills. For example, if they are required to change a tyre in their job, then they must be given the opportunity to do it in their training.

The measurement of interpersonal skills is a much more complex affair. There may be a need to quantify *how well* tasks are carried out, as well as checking that they have actually been completed. A sophisticated checklist detailing indicators of good and poor performance will simplify the process of assessment.

The job behaviour and performance level of assessment identifies whether the training experience has enabled the trainee to perform certain duties. Again, this provides valuable data for the analyst when analysing training needs.

Using Questionnaires

One of the best devices available for use in the training needs analysis process is the questionnaire. It can either take the form of a set of questions contained within some sort of standard social science instrument, or one you or people close to you design for specific information-gathering purposes.

The standard instruments have their pros and cons. Many are available on the market and I will not attempt to review them here. The one thing to bear in mind if you plan to use these instruments is to be sure ahead of time that they will truly help you to obtain the information you require. Finding out about people's aptitudes or their scholastic achievement levels may be useful in general terms. But this kind of information might not be all that helpful to the training needs analysis process.

Questionnaires that you design specifically for training needs purposes can give you much better and more relevant information. But you do need to observe a few precautions and take into account a few factors to obtain the best results.

Designing Questionnaires

In designing your own questionnaires keep the following points in mind:

1. Develop a list of specific questions that will give you important information related to the stage of the training needs analysis process at which you are working.
2. Frame your questions so that your intended respondents will have little room for doubt about the information you seek.
3. Keep your questions short (no more than 17 words if at all possible).
4. Use language that you're sure your respondent will understand.
5. Strive to use positive wording at all times.
6. Keep the number of questions in any one questionnaire under strict control (no more than 25 if at all possible — one rule of

thumb is never to use a questionnaire that will take more than half an hour to answer).

7. Do not attempt to use 'trick' questions.

8. When deciding on the group of people who will respond to your questionnaire, be sure that they are likely to possess the knowledge needed to respond to the questions you ask. (You don't want to indulge in the pooling of ignorance!)

9. Avoid questions that may have negative legal implications.

10. Decide whether or not you want anonymous responses or need to provide for identifying each respondent specifically.

11. When identifying respondents, decide if you'll use code numbers or real names.

12. Avoid questions that really involve two or more questions built into one (separate them!).

13. Do not set up either/or types of questions that involve mutually exclusive ideas (eg 'Do you prefer to have your workbench laid out neatly at the end of your shift, or to leave your work exactly at the point you were when completing your shift? — yes or no?').

14. In general, to improve the quality of the results, seek to have *everyone* in your target group complete the questionnaire. If this is not possible for some reason, arrange for a sample of people that you believe will truly be representative of the target group.

15. As far as possible, avoid having people with a personal interest in the outcome of the training needs analysis process distribute or administer questionnaires on your behalf. Even the most honest and best-intentioned of people can sway things inadvertently.

16. Whenever possible, test newly-constructed questionnaires on selected test groups before actually using them. The support staff involved with your analysis can often help here, and will usually be glad to do so.

17. Avoid asking questions about information you can find out readily by other means (eg consulting a book or a computer database).

18. Put some effort into making sure that your questionnaire has an attractive and professional look to it. Your choice of typeface, paper colour and texture, and ink colour can make a difference here. So too can your use of blank space to help the respondent see your questions clearly set out. Additionally, you might consider the use of some type of cover for your questionnaire or set of questionnaires.

19. Ensure that you have some kind of 'authority endorsement' for introducing your questionnaire (eg 'This is part of the ongoing study authorized by Mr. Quentin Jones, president of Dingbat Marbles').

The types of questions you use can have an important bearing on your results. Will one-word answers such as 'yes' or 'no' be enough? Or do you need questions that will give you answers with a little more depth? The two samples (Figure 6.2 and Figure 6.3) may help you clarify your thinking here.

Examine each of the following statements, then enter a tick under 'True' if you consider the statement true, or under 'False' if you consider it untrue.

True   False

The training I received was relevant to my job   ❏   ❏

Figure 6.2 *True-false question sample*

In the true-false questionnaires, vary the order of true and false responses a little. Avoid a succession of true-false-true-false all the way through. And keep in mind that you don't have to have an equal number of each.

Open-ended questions, such as the one shown at Figure 6.3, in which you invite the respondent to give sentence, paragraph or essay-type answers, can give you much valuable information. People are likelier to loosen up their thinking and to say things you'll find useful, without always realizing they're doing so. But such questions demand a lot of your time afterwards to read and assess.

Think carefully about each of the following questions, then respond in the way that makes most sense to you.

1. Which areas of yòur job would you like included in a training programme?
2. Are there any tasks which you have found to be particularly difficult?

Figure 6.3 *Open-ended question sample*

In analysing the answers to open-ended questions you can use a 'key term' approach. Using this approach you look for words that are the same or are similar in meaning. Keeping track of how often they occur can give you important indications of respondent views, even if the respondents did not clearly articulate those views.

Forced-choice questions (see Figure 6.4) can help to move the respondent from the fence-sitting position, thus giving you a better idea of the tendencies or the thinking in a given respondent or a given group. Some respondents, given forced-choice questions, will mark in their middle positions anyway! But, for the most part, they will make their choices, unless they honestly cannot understand the question you're posing.

Respond to each of the following questions by checking under SA, A, D, or SD (SA = strongly agree; A - agree; D = disagree; SD = strongly disagree).

	SA	A	D	SD
1. Good communication skills are essential in order to be effective in your job.	[ ]	[ ]	[ ]	[ ]
2. It is not necessary to have a wide technical background to be effective in the current role.	[ ]	[ ]	[ ]	[ ]

etc.

Figure 6.4 *Forced-choice question sample*

In general, when you're using forced-choice questions remember to use even numbers for setting out the choices. Four such choices works well. When you use odd numbers such as three or five choices, people have a tendency to choose the middle one.

Consider each of the following tasks. Prioritize those which you found to be the most difficult. Use a *1* to indicate the most difficult task; a *2* for the second most difficult, and so on until you have assigned a priority number to each task on the list. Use a priority number only once.

	Priority
1. Allocating work to subordinates	[ ]
2. Conducting staff appraisal interviews	[ ]
3. Dealing with letters of complaint	[ ]
4. Planning work schedules	[ ]
5. Controlling departmental budgets	[ ]

Figure 6.5 *Priority-ordering sample*

Priority-ordering questions or statements can often prove helpful to your research, although you have to be careful here not to use too many statements. Keeping to a maximum of ten is a good idea.

In the priority-ordering approach you set out a number of statements and then invite the respondent to order them from top to bottom in terms of her or his preferences (and be careful to state that he or she must use each priority number only once!) In giving instructions for this type of instrument, be careful when using numbers to indicate whether lower numbers are higher priority choices or lower. This approach may be useful when trying to establish the 'need to know' and the 'nice to know' content of training. People may be asked to prioritize their job tasks in terms of difficulty, importance and frequency.

In analysing the responses to priority-ordering questionnaires, usually matrix sheets are important for setting out the responses for each questionnaire. This normally enables you to capture all the response information on one sheet of paper.

The sample matrix shown at Figure 6.6 shows how you would set out a hypothetical matrix for the results obtained from a priority-ordering questionnaire that had involved five statements, with 1 being the highest priority number selection. This matrix is made out for six respondents. The 'Q' stands for 'question' or 'statement number'. The 'R' stands for 'respondent number'.

R / Q	1	2	3	4	5	6		Totals	Overall Priorities
1	1	2	3	2	2	1		11	1
2	3	1	2	3	1	2		12	2
3	5	4	4	5	5	3		26	5
4	4	5	5	1	4	5		24	4
5	2	3	1	4	3	4		17	3
				Check	totals			90	15

Figure 6.6 *Matrix for priority-ordered questionnaire*

You don't have to include the check totals, but they can help, especially with larger samplings, to ensure that the responses have been tabulated correctly on the matrix. In the case of a 5-statement priority-ordered questionnaire the check total for the questionnaire itself is 15 (1 + 2 + 3 + 4 + 5 = 15). It's not foolproof, but as a quick check it will usually discover if the respondent used all the priority numbers in responding to the questionnaire. This number appears as the check total on our matrix for the final 'overall priorities' total. That check total, of course, will be the same as that for each individual questionnaire.

You total up the number responses for each statement row in turn and enter this total in the 'totals' column. In this case, because 1 was our highest priority number, the lowest total would receive a 1 to indicate that row number has the highest overall priority. The next lowest total would receive a 2, and so on.

The check total for the 'totals' column is 90. This comes from multiplying the number of respondents (6) by the individual questionnaire check totals.

In some cases the totals for a given statement row will come out the same, so the priority number will be the same. Suppose this occurred giving us two rows with the same totals at the 2 priority level. Here you'd assign a priority of 2 to each of the row statements. Then carry on with the rest of your priority numbering. Note here that your check total for the priorities column will no longer work, so rely on the check total for all the individual totals.

Analysing the priority-ordering types of questionnaires can involve a bit of work, but it can give you an interesting insight into the thinking or the preferences of a given group of people. The resulting matrix is also convenient to handle in meetings or as an attachment in your final training needs analysis process report.

You might also use a *rating scale* kind of questionnaire. The rating scale often makes it easier for people to note their degrees of agreement or disagreement more finely (see Figure 6.7).

Please examine each of the following statements and then indicate the degree to which you support or do not support what it says by making a vertical mark on the scale that indicates your opinion.

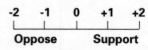

Conducting training in your skill at Breckenridge Polytechnic. etc.

-2   -1   0   +1   +2

Oppose   Support

Figure 6.7 *Rating scale sample*

In setting out questions using the rating scale method, deliberately phrase a few of your questions to bring out opposition or negative responses as opposed to support or positive responses. You want to guard against any tendency the respondent may have to respond on the same side of the scale all the way through.

In using the rating scale approach, you do not have to use the same words on the scale itself all the way through. You might vary things a little (eg use scales of agree — disagree; don't include — include; aware — unaware, and so on). Similarly, if you do decide to use the same rating words, you might set them out at the top of the questionnaire and not repeat them for each individual rating line. Also, you may decide to dispense with numbers, and note appropriate words at each mark on the scale.

We made a special case of showing the matrix approach to tabulating the results of the priority-ordered questionnaire. You can tabulate the other types of questionnaires, for the most part, in a more straightforward way. The main thing is to try to have one reconciliation sheet on which you can show the generalized result of all the individual responses you have received. This will enable you to analyse the results more readily, as well as to use them more comfortably in various kinds of presentations.

Other questionnaire structures do exist, but you have enough here to go on, or at least to use as idea-joggers to design your own when that seems the proper route.

Administering Questionnaires

The way you administer or distribute questionnaires is important. If you use the post, for instance, you run the risk that others will intervene in some way, thereby 'contaminating' the results you'll obtain. You also increase the risk that not everyone in your sample group will respond.

If at all possible, arrange to be present to introduce and distribute questionnaires directly to the respondents. As part of this process, work to ensure that this transaction takes place directly between you and the respondents. You don't want a plant manager or some other authority figure pacing up and down nervously or threateningly while people respond to the questions you've crafted.

Make sure that your respondents feel comfortable with the idea of asking you questions at any time while they're filling out the questionnaire or questionnaires. This way, you'll lower the possibility of misinterpretation. You may also find out additional useful details that you hadn't thought to ask for in the questionnaire itself.

115

While administering a questionnaire, circulate around the room a little. But don't appear impatient or rushed for time, or move around too mechanically or too frequently.

The Respondent Mix

As a general rule, when people are responding in a group to a given questionnaire, they will work most comfortably and most accurately when they're alongside people they know and who are at the same level in the organization. Bosses or strangers might distract their thinking, or cause them to be less honest in their responses than they should be.

Responding Hierarchies

In some cases, the subject matter of a questionnaire may make it reasonable to administer the same questionnaire to different groups at different levels in the organization. For instance, you might want to include the bosses of your target group. Keep in mind the diagram at Figure 6.8 as you think through the particular hierarchy you might wish to involve.

When you make yourself think deliberately about the kind of hierarchy you might work with for any given questionnaire, you'll sometimes force out surprising and potentially quite useful additional sources to tap. A little creativity here can be a good thing.

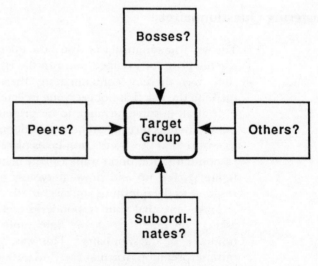

Figure 6.8 *Responding hierarchy*

Thinking about your responding hierarchy can also be a good thing to do when using devices other than questionnaires to gather or work with your information.

By using a hierarchical approach you can often spot areas of information or communication breakdown, including problems in the quality of the replies you may have received using other methods earlier in the training needs analysis process. Look closely for such response anomalies. They will often be important, and sometimes crucially so.

TRAINER'S TIPS

1. Remain creative in your search for the information sources you might use.
2. Always be on the lookout for 'key communicators' in the organization. These people have often stored up surprisingly good information bases that they're happy to share with the right treatment.
3. At all times look for the self-serving items of information people may choose to give you — these may be distortions of the complete facts.
4. In your research look for ways in which one information source can logically lead you to another information source.
5. Plan and be organized, but remain cautious about 'imposing structure' on the people from whom you wish to receive information.
6. Every now and then do a 'bias check' on yourself to ensure that you are not inadvertently shaping your information to support your own preferred outcomes.
7. No matter who you're dealing with, make it plain to that person that you respect him or her and the views he or she expresses.
8. When people communicate with you confidentially, always respect the promises you make to guard that confidentiality.
9. When working with groups of people, always look for ways of making the group feel comfortable — strive to help them see you as trustworthy.
10. At all times remain clear about your own agenda. This will help you guard against being subtly or unduly swayed towards someone's favoured viewpoint.
11. Keep first-class records of all the information you gather, no matter what technique you've used to gather it.

Related Work

Sometimes you may wish to come back to a given respondent group to give them general feedback about their responses and, perhaps, to gain further understanding of their feelings or information. At other times, you may wish to use questionnaires as part of the structure of an interview session. Sometimes too, one questionnaire and its results may beget another questionnaire for a different group, perhaps one you hadn't thought of before.

Never consider the use of questionnaires as something to be done in isolation. Always be looking for ways to relate them to other work, or to use them as part of other work.

The Nominal Group Method

This is a means of running a meeting to bring out information in an open, confidential, and free-wheeling atmosphere. In effect, it's a form of controlled brain storming.

Use this method with a group you've identified as likely to provide you with the information you need. This could be an organizational work group or a group you put together based on the expertise of the people involved. You can also use it, at times, with groups of fellow analysts as you work through the significance of the information you've uncovered at various stages of the training needs analysis process.

The nominal group approach is particularly appropriate when you wish people to come up with ideas or points of information, but suspect that they might hold back from openly divulging what they have to say. This may occur because they know other people at the meeting may have divergent or hostile reactions. Naturally, if such people have higher rank in the organization, their presence could well be intimidating.

The nominal group process makes it possible for people to have their say anonymously, at least in the early stages. It also helps to avoid having people jumping to given ideas too quickly because of the status or communicating power of one person or a minority of people.

Use the nominal group method early in your analytical work or later on to help refine things. In some cases you may have the same group go through this process two or more times, perhaps to deal with the points emerging from earlier sessions.

Because this method involves a group operating in key steps, the easiest way to explain it is to describe these steps, which are:

1. Clarify for the group the objectives you wish them to help you meet during this session (eg 'We want to identify the most important training needs for our branch at this point in time').
2. Ask each person to write down on a small sheet of paper his/her response to your first question or direction (eg Write down

the training needs for our branch that stand out in your mind right now). Allot five minutes for this first writing task.

3. Point out to everyone that they must not talk to each other during each writing phase.

4. Collect all the sheets of paper after five minutes and note their contents on a board or overhead projector. Where you have the same point coming up more than once, use tick marks to indicate additional listings.

5. Allow everyone a couple of minutes to view the total list of points.

6. Conduct several more rounds of writing down training needs until all the needs within the group have been noted. Give everyone a chance to view the total listing between each writing session.

7. When you have all the points listed in response to your directions or questions, identify their priorities for the group by asking each person on his/her own to write down privately a priority ranking for each need being displayed.

8. Collect the sheets of paper with the priority rankings and work these rankings through on the board.

9. For finer identification of priorities, eliminate (for the time being) items with the lowest scores, then ask everyone to list their priorities again for the remaining items. In keeping with this, you may want to write the points out again according to their overall priority ranking.

10. You can eliminate low scoring items in a succession of priority-setting rounds, until you have a clear picture of the priorities for all the remaining items.

11. After you've received the answers to the questions you've asked or the responses to the directions you've given, ask each person in the group to write down his/her general comments about these questions or directions.

12. Promise the group you will send out summary copies of the needs and comments brought out in this session.

The nominal group method allows people comfortably to participate in a needs identification or analysis session without worrying about the group pressures of particular individuals who may delight in using group manipulation tactics. You can bring out points that might otherwise not have received attention because they were buried under somebody's favourite topic steamroller.

The priority setting part of this method is useful, but you have to make sure it's handled confidentially. By doing so you can probe into areas of importance without the usual group communication distortions.

The steps given here can be varied to meet different needs. You might, for instance, encourage open discussion at key intervals. The main thing is to ensure you control the session sufficiently to bring out information as objectively as possible. It's especially important that you do not 'contaminate' the process yourself by showing signs of favouritism for your own preferred topics.

The nominal group method is a flexible one. You can use it in a number of different settings for many different purposes. Make sure, when you do use it, that you take charge of the process in a fully effective way. This benefits everyone.

The Delphi Technique

This technique, which originated with the Rand Corporation (although some might argue it originated with the ancient Greeks), builds in many of the advantages of the nominal group method, but can be used more easily over a longer period of time with a large number of people in different locations. Again, like the nominal group method, this technique requires care in handling for it to work properly.

In essence the Delphi technique involves these steps:

1. Identify the key training analysis questions to which you wish to receive answers.
2. Select the best survey population for giving you answers to your questions.
3. Canvas your selected population to secure their cooperation in answering the questionnaire you will send them. Tell them you will observe complete confidentiality in working with their responses. Give each person a basic outline of the Delphi technique process. (Memos, letters, and phone calls should all be used here.)
4. Phrase your questions in a clear questionnaire format.
5. Send a copy of your questionnaire to each member of the selected survey population (attach a reminder noting the date by which you need to receive their responses).
6. Ensure you receive responses from all or nearly all of your survey population (make phone calls, pay visits and so on, to obtain the responses).
7. Pull together the responses you receive in a rational summary of information (for more open-ended types of questions, use key term analysis to identify key or common thrusts of information).

8. Based on the responses to your first questionnaire, build a second questionnaire to filter and fine tune the responses.
9. Send out the second questionnaire to the same population.
10. Repeat steps 6 and 7.
11. If necessary, send out third and fourth questionnaires to refine your response information as far as possible. (In some cases you may go beyond four, but make sure it's really important if you do.)
12. Give each person in your survey population a copy of your summary report of the key items of information identified with their help. If practical, let them know the significance of this information to the overall training needs analysis process.

Word the questions you plan to use as specifically and unambiguously as possible. For the most part design them to bring out short answers (although a few open-ended questions are always wise additions). Always give a reasonable amount of space at the end of your questionnaire for people to add in their thoughts or comments in an unstructured way.

Whatever type of questionnaire you decide to use, double check to make sure that it's appropriate to the questions you need to delve into. Perhaps the comments of your colleagues would help here. A practice survey with a small group of volunteers could be invaluable in helping you to put the final polish on your questionnaire.

Your sample population

In selecting your survey population, look for people who are most likely to know the answers you're looking for and who are likely to have some real impact on implementing the results of your training analysis work. Here again you need to look for decision makers, especially key decision makers. (Mere opinion givers won't necessarily be of help to you here, although they may be able to help you with the initial questionnaire design.)

Keep your survey population within manageable bounds — up to twenty well-selected people. If you get into larger numbers you'll have to start working with full-scale statistical analysis techniques.

Your results are statistically dependent on the validity of the sample you select (are these the people whose opinions are truly relevant to the needs being examined?). Your results are also dependent statistically on the degree of response within your sample group (100% is wonderful).

In selecting the people to include in your sample, take into account these important questions:

1. Is the person a key decision maker for the area involved (a boss or professional of some kind)?

121

2. Is this individual familiar with the workings of the area you are investigating?
3. Is this person a 'key communicator' (ie a person generally considered to be in the know and with whom others in the group regularly share information).
4. Does this person have a subject knowledge base for the area you are examining (a former employee or a student)?
5. Is this person up-to-date on the needs of the work area being examined?

You need not select only those people for whom you can answer 'yes' to *all* these questions. A 'yes' answer on even one could help in some cases, but bear in mind the question of your total sample size. If you have an overwhelming number of potential respondents to deal with at first, try using these questions to whittle down the number. The more 'yes' responses you give a particular individual, the more important it is for you to include that person in your sample.

In putting together your sample group, you may have to interview a number of people to find out for sure who your best information resources are likely to be. This takes time. Prepare clear questions in order to identify the people you need.

Beware of self-selected sample groups. Many people might volunteer to take part in your survey because they think it's their job to do so or because it sounds interesting to them. This does not in itself mean they know what they're talking about. They could just be full of untested opinions and theories.

In keeping with the focal point of good training needs analysis work, which is actual or future on-the-job performance, you need people who are truly likely to have a close and accurate perspective on that performance. This is not likely to include self-appointed experts.

Beware also of using sample groups composed of people who are conveniently 'available'. They may or may not be the right people for you to survey. Again, keep the five selecting questions in mind.

When your response level is less than 100%, you have to be careful. But even a 50% response level is useful provided the people responding give you sufficient depth and breadth in the organization you are dealing with, although this still leaves you with some large question marks.

In general, your survey results are likely to be seriously flawed if you're working with a response level of less than 80%. It is partly for this reason that it is so important to follow up on the questionnaires you send out.

Key term analysis

In using the Delphi technique, the key thrusts of information given to you by your respondents are important. For this purpose you need to engage in key term analysis, which involves identifying words or phrases that seem to cover the important issues repeatedly raised by different people. Consider the following hypothetical statements made by four different people:

- '... the parts we need for final assembly often arrive late ...'
- '... perhaps management could arrange for us to receive parts earlier in the final assembly area ...'
- '... often we haven't been able to complete our work on time because we don't have everything we need soon enough ...'
- '... somebody screws up arrival times for delivery of the parts we need ...'

What is the theme running through these statements? It's 'lateness of parts delivery', so this term itself could become a key term in your review of responses. After reading over a few more responses you might decide you want to reword this term positively, so it could become 'ensuring the timely arrival of parts'.

You can use this same process for other themes you identify. Gradually, you'll have a set of key terms, and this set might lead to important breakthroughs in your thinking and the thinking of others with whom you may be working.

When preparing yourself to look for key terms, it might be useful to equip yourself with a deck of index cards. For each questionnaire you review in turn, mark in a term as mentioned by the respondent (eg 'Many of our people are unsure of their required job duties'). You might write this out in full, or summarize it as, 'Lack of clarity about job duties'. The summarizing process might, of course, lead you directly to a key term that will work readily for other statements by other respondents.

Each term mentioned in the first questionnaire you deal with should receive its own index card. For subsequent questionnaires you can start looking for common threads. If, for instance, someone else mentions the same issue in almost the same words enter a '+' to indicate that you've now got two mentions of that key term.

When someone mentions something close to, but not exactly the same as, a point you've already noted on an index card, you might note it on the same index card; in so doing, write it out in full or in accurate summary form. Later on you might decide it's worded more accurately for the issue people seem to be touching on, and revise your key terms as you go.

When you have a complete set of filled-out index cards, go over them to group them according to areas of common concern. You might find certain terms come to mind that capture the essence of the factors you're grouping. Test this term in your own mind and with others before deciding to use it. If it holds up, by all means start using it. It could represent an even better refinement of your key term.

In some cases you might identify factors in your review that none of your respondents had specifically stated but are there implicitly. In effect, you could end up with 'emergent' key terms.

Key term analysis is time-consuming and demands a lot of patience as well as investigative insight. But it plays a fundamental role in bringing out important issues and clarifying them as objectively as possible.

Dealing with the outcomes

The Delphi technique offers you a powerful means of gaining good information for thorough training needs analysis work. It is not a 'quicky solution' by any stretch of the imagination, but it does offer you a structured process to filter out good information. Further, with its graduated workings, it brings you into a position that enables you to discover and work with real training needs in the sharpest possible light.

The built-in confidentiality aspects of the Delphi technique are essential to its successful use. Take care, for instance, not to inadvertently pit one respondent against another by saying something like, 'Well, you know, Peter Markov thought we should do more training in the area of computerized billings'. This kind of comment is an open invitation to set organizational politics into motion.

Pulling together in a report of some kind all the information you gather in using the Delphi technique is important. In writing this report bear in mind the need to set out your methodology clearly for your readers. This includes identifying the members of your sample group (but not their individual responses).

In some cases it may be worthwhile to put your information into a perspective that involves more sophisticated statistical methodology. You could do this for sharpening the results of particular survey areas, to produce more impact on those people you wish to influence.

The Delphi technique can provide you with a lot of answers for your analytical work. It gives you a rationale for the training decisions you think are necessary. It also gives you a good base from which to deal with different stages of the total training needs analysis process.

Using a Dynamic Classification Chart to Sort Information

You can use a dynamic classification chart in almost any kind of business or government work setting. You can key it in to various aspects and various stages of the training needs analysis process. In considering using it, compare its possibilities with the options comparison matrix dealt with in Chapter 4.

The dynamic classification chart has similarities to what is called 'storyboarding' in the entertainment industry. You set out important themes and relate them to sub-themes in order to help the overall process of making sense of a mass of information. It enables you then to tell a coherent 'story' based on your information. It works with one person. But it works especially well with a group of people.

Depending on the area or precise issue you're dealing with, you can use a dynamic classification chart for a day or up to a matter of weeks. In the latter case you might, for instance, have a two-day session once a month for three months.

The dynamic classification chart offers you a means of rationally dealing with a mass of information to classify items within key areas or to set them out in priorities. You can then go on to manipulate that information further, according to additional classifications that suggest themselves 'live'. This often makes it an ideal means of involving a group of people to examine the same information and then react to that information according to their own areas of expertise. When a group uses this approach to sort information, classifications tend to fall into place as a natural part of the process.

One of the key steps in using the dynamic classification chart is to set up a large board (made of any hard material) to which you'll be able to attach small cards or rectangles of paper. You can also plan to use a blank wall for this purpose. Your chart will unfold with cards or paper rectangles being labelled as you or the group note key information points and give them a place on the board or wall.

This is an outline of the step-by-step process to follow in using the dynamic classification chart with a group of people:

1. Identify an area you believe will lend itself to a session focused on classifying points of information dynamically.
2. Select a fully competent coordinator to run the session.
3. Prepare a good supply of index cards or stick-on note pads (5" x 8") in at least three different colours.
4. Make sure you have a large room available where the group can work undisturbed throughout the session (including evenings).

This room requires clear walls or large boards on which you can attach the index cards or stick-on papers as you work.

5. Select a small group of people knowledgeable about the area you wish to examine.
6. If possible, have a number of additional experts available by phone should you need to call them to ask questions during the session.
7. Make sure the group will be available to work with the dynamic classification chart for a couple of days (this may vary, depending on the complexity of the issues you're examining).
8. Give each member of the group a copy of a paper or report showing all the main items of information already established for the area under examination.
9. Explain the basic ground rules for the process including:
   a. The need to keep comments as objective and balanced as possible;
   b. The possibility of changing particular points from one position to another on the developing chart as more information comes out in discussion;
   c. The distinction between items of information and the classifications that may arise for that information.
10. On index cards of a given colour, write the names of the classifications that may already be known and attach these to your display board in a vertical column (and don't worry about order of priority at this stage).
11. Write out all the items of information you now have in horizontal rows running to the left or right of the classifications they seem to fit. Here's where a little dynamism will often come into play. Sometimes, if information doesn't appear to fit existing classifications, the group will create an appropriate classification name after considering an item or two of unclassified information. (Use a different colour for these cards from the colour used for the classification name.)
12. Ask the group to confirm the classifications and their related items of information or from time to time to suggest changes.

The person you select to conduct or facilitate the session is crucial to the success of the process. She or he needs excellent group leadership skills of the non-directive and directive kind. She or he must have the ability to use the right type of facilitation skill as the situation demands, and preferably not have direct personal connections with the general area of information being examined. This helps to ensure leadership that is as objective as possible.

The group must be carefully selected. You want people with excellent

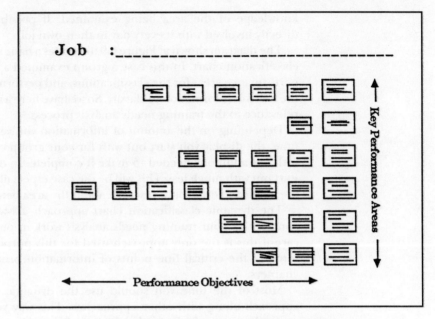

Figure 6.9 *A dynamic classification chart*

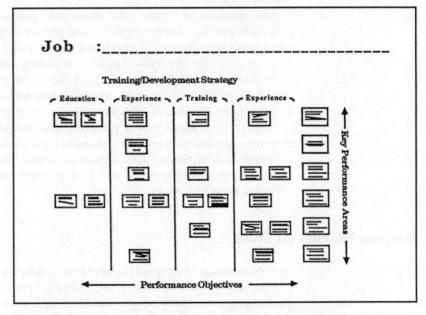

Figure 6.10 *Training/development dynamic classification chart*

knowledge of the area being examined. If possible, they should be directly involved with it every day in their own jobs.

The diagram shown at Figure 6.9 illustrates a basic set up for a dynamic classification chart. In this case a group examined a given job, used key performance areas for the classifications, and performance objectives for the items of information to classify. So we have here a situation with direct relevance to the training needs analysis process.

Depending on the amount of information you've acquired ahead of time, the display you start out with for your group could look like this, with few additions needed to make it complete. In other cases you may start out with much less. This will be the case especially if you haven't had the chance to do a lot of research about the area being considered.

The dynamic classification chart approach allows you, at times, to conduct *all* your training needs analysis work in one session. But take care if this is the only approach used for this purpose. You could lose some of the critical fine points of information brought out in earlier chapters.

Most of the time you should use the dynamic classification chart approach along with other approaches. This way you can cross-check particular items of information and sift things through to the maximum possible extent.

The diagram at Figure 6.10 shows how you can use this charting process to put together a comprehensive picture of the training/development processes required in a given training needs analysis situation. This could give you an important means of analysing training needs.

At times the classifications you work out in the dynamic classification process help you select a particular education or training session to use. In some cases this means helping to design those sessions to fill the bill.

This process offers you a powerful and flexible means of sorting through complex information to develop clear pictures of classifications, priorities and, at times, likely courses of action. Be sure to think about using this process whenever you find yourself struggling to sort out complex areas and issues.

Keeping Yourself on Track

In organizations of all types the problem of keeping yourself on track in conducting various aspects of the training needs analysis process is a challenging one. Many people and external forces exist that fly against the logic and quality of effective analysis. For your analysis to prove worthwhile, it needs shielding from these potentially disruptive factors.

You can't challenge everyone in sight with straight power tactics (unless you're in a very powerful position). You have to focus on keeping your own mind as clear and directed as possible, while convincing or teaching the people you're in contact with to appreciate and support the finer points of the training needs analysis process.

Without effective, clear-headed attention to the fine points on your own part, top quality work becomes all but impossible. It too easily slides into providing justification for what other people want, regardless of whether or not their wants actually address specific and real organizational needs.

The full-scale job of analysing is not an easy one. But it is a vitally important one. You won't always get the chance to do it right. But it's most important that you make every effort, no matter what the circumstances, to get it as right as possible.

Perhaps you can't perform organizational miracles. You can, however, provide substantial organizational contributions through good analytical work, and so much depends on your own strength and integrity. These attributes are essential to the results you must achieve.

Using the Techniques

You may or may not use all the techniques or methods we've gone over in this chapter. At times, the points we've gone over in earlier chapters will suffice for your purposes. This applies especially to those brought out in Chapter 4.

The real key to being a good analyst for identifying and analysing training needs isn't so much the ability to carry out a particular approach with a reasonable degree of proficiency. It's being able to work out, set up, and apply the particular approach right for the situation, people, and issues you're dealing with. This approach will vary from one analysis project to the next.

Good information is vital to all of this. Think about the methods, ideas and techniques brought out in this chapter, and apply them whenever and wherever you believe they're likely to help.

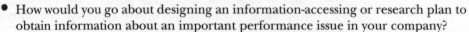

► QUESTIONS FOR THE ANALYST ◄

- How would you go about designing an information-accessing or research plan to obtain information about an important performance issue in your company?
- During the last meeting you attended, did your mind wander, or did you find yourself taking in all the details?
- In what specific ways can you improve your own interview skills?
- Think of people you deal with regularly whom you might consider clients. How can you go about improving the way you deal with them?
- Think of an area where you need to gather information. What kind of questionnaire could you design to help you obtain that information?
- Identify a specific group of people whom you might use as a sample group for information. What prejudices or inadvertent distortions would you have to guard against with that group?
- What specific situations can you think of where you might actually use the nominal group method?
- Would the Delphi technique be practical to use in your company?
- How might the dynamic classification chart approach help you sort out an information situation you must deal with soon?
- What are the specific ways you can keep yourself on track while engaged in gathering detailed information for a given project?

Appendix:

Personal Evaluation Inventory for Skill in the Training Needs Analysis Process

This evaluation inventory will help you to examine your own abilities related to working effectively with your clients in conducting training needs analysis work. By responding as honestly as you can to each statement, you will provide yourself with the basis for a personal action plan you can implement to improve your future interactions.

Beside each statement is a short scale. Use this scale to show your own personal degree of competence for the area described.

> 1. Very little competence
>
> 2. Some competence
>
> 3. Moderate competence
>
> 4. High competence

And remember, this evaluation is for your own use in your own way.

	Competence level			
	1	2	3	4
1. Making sure I've worked through my plan for dealing with my clients before beginning any key part of the training needs analysis process.	❏	❏	❏	❏
2. Ensuring that I greet all clients in a friendly and business-like manner.	❏	❏	❏	❏
3. Interacting well with people, including dealing effectively with their questions.				
4. Finding out exactly who my key decision maker or authorizing person is for each stage of the training needs analysis process.	❏	❏	❏	❏
5. Discreetly monitoring the actions and responses of people to gauge the effectiveness of my communications with them.	❏	❏	❏	❏
6. Working through a complete Training Needs Analysis Process Plan, and being able to explain this plan to others.	❏	❏	❏	❏
7. Ensuring that I provide people with clear explanations of the various technical terms I use with them.	❏	❏	❏	❏
8. Finding various ways to gain commitment from people to ensure the value of my training needs analysis work with them — setting up my training needs analysis contract.	❏	❏	❏	❏
9. When necessary, producing task outlines for given tasks within a job or work area.	❏	❏	❏	❏
10. Producing performance objectives when needed.	❏	❏	❏	❏
11. Constructing performance sets to demonstrate clear relationships of performance objectives within a work area.	❏	❏	❏	❏
12. Working successfully within the organizational climate of any work group, department or organization I'm dealing with.	❏	❏	❏	❏
13. As required, working effectively on my own or as part of a team when engaged in any aspect of the training needs analysis process.	❏	❏	❏	❏

	Competence level			
	1	2	3	4

14. When necessary, producing a research plan to detail how and where the information required for carrying out the training needs analysis process will be obtained. ☐ ☐ ☐ ☐

15. When needed, arranging to observe work being done in the workplace, and observing such work objectively and accurately. ☐ ☐ ☐ ☐

16. Obtaining permission, as necessary, to interview key employees, supervisors or managers. ☐ ☐ ☐ ☐

17. Having the capacity to carry out effective interviews as needed to gather and assess information. ☐ ☐ ☐ ☐

18. Knowing the key issues of human motivation to be on the lookout for in my work with any organization. ☐ ☐ ☐ ☐

19. Conducting and showing others how to conduct job performance audits when required to carefully identify performance discrepancies in the workplace. ☐ ☐ ☐ ☐

20. When the situation demands it, dealing diplomatically and carefully with the issue of what has caused performance discrepancies. ☐ ☐ ☐ ☐

21. Understanding how to analyse training needs to ensure that they are classified properly, and are then linked to the right kinds of training or education solutions. ☐ ☐ ☐ ☐

22. When needed, being able to produce training objectives, and to show other people how to produce them. ☐ ☐ ☐ ☐

23. When required, grouping training objectives together within training modules, and producing objectives for those modules. ☐ ☐ ☐ ☐

24. Placing the emphasis in my work on obtaining competent employee performance in the work areas examined, not on selecting people to attend existing training programmes. ☐ ☐ ☐ ☐

	Competence level			
	1	2	3	4
25. As needed, producing action appraisals to logically plan out key stages and areas of the training needs analysis process.	❐	❐	❐	❐
26. Remaining attentive to all forms of communication and information flow available to me.	❐	❐	❐	❐
27. When required, producing a factors chart to clearly arrange the pro and con factors for a given training needs analysis objective or other proposed course of action.	❐	❐	❐	❐
28. Producing an options comparison matrix when this will help the decision-making process.	❐	❐	❐	❐
29. Setting out a basic PERT chart when this will likely help the planning process being worked out.	❐	❐	❐	❐
30. Being able as needed to produce good questionnaires to meet information-gathering needs.	❐	❐	❐	❐
31. Using the nominal group technique for running an information-gathering or assessing meeting with skill and confidence.	❐	❐	❐	❐
32. Having the capacity, when suited to the situation, to employ the Delphi technique to gather and assess information.	❐	❐	❐	❐
33. Using the dynamic classification chart process with skill on my own, as part of a team, or as a group leader.	❐	❐	❐	❐
34. Ending each session with a client on the right note.	❐	❐	❐	❐
35. Using the options comparison matrix effectively to help sort through different courses of action for meeting training or performance needs.	❐	❐	❐	❐
36. When appropriate, writing performance needs reports that clearly lay out the organization's performance needs, and specify the exact areas in which training will make a difference.	❐	❐	❐	❐

Self-evaluation can sometimes involve a little pain. But, in the long run it will give you many benefits. By answering these questions as honestly as you can, you're giving yourself invaluable information to use in bettering your work with training needs analysis. Responding to these questions from time to time on a continuing basis will ensure that your work continues to improve into the future. And this will benefit not only the organizations you deal with, but you as well.

Selected Readings

These books are either cited in the text or additional ones you may wish to consult concerning the training needs analysis process and related areas.

Applegarth, Michael (1991) *How to Take a Training Audit*. London: Kogan Page.

Boyett, Joseph H and Conn, Henry P (1991). *Workplace 2000*. New York: Dutton.

Chaplin, JP (1975) *Dictionary of Psychology*. New York: Dell Publishing.

Friesen, Paul A (1971) *Designing Instruction*. Ottawa: Friesen, Kaye & Associates.

Gagné, Robert M (1971) 'Identifying Objectives: Task Description' in *Instructional Design: Readings*. Englewood Cliffs, New Jersey.

Gagné, Robert M (1971) 'The Reasons for Specifying Objectives' in *Instructional Design: Readings*. Englewood Cliffs, New Jersey.

Hersey, Paul and Blanchard, Kenneth H (1977) *Management of Organizational Behavior*. Englewood Cliffs: Prentice-Hall.

Herzberg, F(1966) *Work and The Nature of Man*. New York: World Publishing.

Kenney, JPJ and Donnelly, EL (1972) *Manpower Training and Development*. London: George G Harrap.

Kryspin, William J (1974) *Writing Behavioral Objectives*. Minneapolis, Minnesota: Burgess Publishing Company.

Mager, Robert F (1990) *Measuring Instructional Results*. London: Kogan Page.

Mager, Robert F (1990) *Preparing Instructional Objectives*. London: Kogan Page.

Mager, Robert F and Beach, Kenneth M (1967) *Developing Vocational Instruction*. Belmont, California: Lake Publishing.

Mager, Robert F and Pipe, Peter (1970) *Analyzing Performance Problems.* Belmont, California: Pearon-Pitman.

Maslow, AH (1962) *Toward a Psychology of Being.* Princeton, NJ: D.Van Nostrand.

Morrison, James H (1979) 'Determining Training Needs' in *Training and Development Handbook.* New York: McGraw-Hill Book Company.

Mouly, George J (1963) *The Science of Educational Research.* New York: American Book Company.

Naisbitt, John and Aburdene, Patricia (1985) *Re-inventing the Corporation.* New York: Warner Books, Inc.

Pascale, Richard Tanner and Athos, Anthony G (1981) *The Art of Japanese Management.* New York: Simon and Schuster.

Peters, Thomas J and Waterman, Robert H (1982) *In Search of Excellence.* New York: Harper & Row.

Peterson, Robyn (1992) *Managing Successful Learning.* London: Kogan Page.

Russo, J Edward and Schoemaker, Paul JH (1989) *Decision Traps.* New York: Doubleday.

Senge, Peter M (1990) *The Fifth Discipline.* New York: Doubleday.

Singer, Edwin J and Ramsden, John (1969) *The Practical Approach to Skills Analysis.* London: McGraw-Hill.

Skinner, BF (1968) *The Technology of Teaching.* New York: Appleton-Century-Crofts.

Smith, Barry J and Delaye, Brian L (1983) *How to be An Effective Trainer.* New York: John Wiley & Sons, Inc.

Suessmuth, Patrick (1986) *Training Ideas Found Useful Part 3.* Winnipeg: Paracan Publications.

Townsend, Patrick L (1986) *Commit to Quality.* New York: John Wiley & Sons, Inc.

The International Board of Standards for Training, Performance and Instruction (1986) *Instructional Design Competencies.* Iowa City: The University of Iowa.

Index